Hardanger
with Pizzazz

by Ina Orr

GPL **GEORGESON** PUBLISHING LIMITED

Published by Georgeson Publishing Limited

**P.O. Box 100-667, North Shore Mail Centre,
New Zealand 1330.**

Email: gpl@georgeson.com.au, Web Site: www.georgeson.co.nz

We have made every effort to ensure that these instructions are accurate and complete. We cannot, however, be responsible for human error, typographical mistakes, or variations in individual work.

ISBN No. 0-9582105-9-4

Editor:	Prue Georgeson
Photography:	Maria Sainsbury
Charts:	Prue Georgeson
Illustrations and Layout:	Andreena Buckton, Noodle Design Corp.

contents

Introduction   4

Hardanger - a brief history   5

Before you begin
    tacking   9
    charts   10

Stitch diagrams
    Starting and finishing   11
    Kloster blocks   12
    Satin stitch   14
    Buttonhole edging stitch   15
    Eyelets   17
    Cable stitch   18
    Cutting threads in preparation for fillings   20
    Intro to needle lace filling stitches and
        step movement   21
    Needle weaving   22
    Overcaste bars (wrapped bars)   23
    Woven bars and picots   24
    Woven bars with dove's eye filling   25
    Wrapped bars with Greek Cross filling   26
    Oblique loop filling with a twist   27
    Antique hem stitch   28
    Mitre corners   29

Hardanger square box   30

Oblong box   35

Small blue mat   40

Christmas runner   45

Handerchief sachet   51

Travelling hussif & accessories   56

Jewellery roll   70

Workbag & accessories   84

Introduction

Embroidery is the one passion that has been with me for as long as I can remember - certainly since about the age of five. As a trained teacher, I have been able to develop and pass on my embroidery knowledge to others. I have taught children and adults, beginners and those with experience also including distance teaching by correspondence. I have helped in the administration and establishment of embroidery guilds including the development of teaching programs for new members. Although I love all forms of embroidery, I have found the study of the development of Hardanger most fascinating. I hope this book will encourage you to become familiar with this technique and my wish is that you will come to enjoy working Hardanger as much as I do.

I enjoy the rhythm I create when working the satin stitch pattern and Kloster blocks and find it very soothing. Then as the work progresses and you start to see the play of light on the threads your enjoyment increases and spurs you on to the finish. The intricate patterns formed with needle weaving add to the enjoyment of a piece of work and now with the introduction of coloured threads a whole new dimension to Hardanger has been introduced.

In this book you will find that most projects have used the hand-dyed threads known as Caron 'Watercolours' and 'Wildflowers'. These threads come in a multitude of variegated colours, some giving a very subtle colour change while others give a more dramatic variation.
If the colours suggested do not appeal to you, do not hesitate to change and experiment as colour plays such an important part in our lives today.

While being mindful of the hundreds of years of careful and accurate training in the Hardanger technique that has been passed down to us, we have the freedom of thought and the ability to use old ideas and add today's wide range of materials to produce today, heirlooms for tomorrow and in the process, enhance this enjoyable technique.

I encourage you to produce - *Hardanger with Pizzazz*

Ina Orr,
Auckland, New Zealand, 2003

Hardanger - a brief history

The origins of Hardanger are difficult to trace as this form of embroidery came from isolated and relatively unknown areas of Norway. Embroidery has been worked in Scandinavian countries since the bronze age about 4000 years ago and many of the traditional Hardanger motifs can be found on ancient garments originating from the Middle East.

The Vikings, followed by the Crusaders of the Middle Ages, brought to the relatively isolated areas of Norway, techniques such as Danish Hedebo and Italian Reticella work. This resulted in a change in stitching as it introduced cut work with fillings and thus began the development of Hardanger.

It was some time between 1650 and 1850 that Hardanger as we know it today began to develop. However the true origins of this technique are relatively obscure as very little is known about the technique prior to 1800. Early lessons in embroidery were taught by word of mouth and passed in this way from one generation to the next.

Indications are that Hardängersom originated from two very isolated western areas of Norway: Hardanger and Voss. It is also thought that Hardanger was being worked in Rindaleu in Nordmore in the 1790's. When the lavish Victorian era arrived in Norway, the Hardanger technique expanded from isolated areas into the urban centres with more people learning to stitch. At the same time the traditional festive decorated items stitched were extended with the addition of table linen and doilies.

All the earliest examples of Hardanger were worked on fine white linen, in white thread. Some of the linens had a thread count as high as 50 threads per inch. There are not many early surviving examples of this technique but there is one piece which can be seen in the Vesterhein Museum in Decorah, Iowa which was produced in the 18th century. These fine pieces of work were very delicate airy pieces, almost completely covered in stitches. Because of this it is often classified as a 'whitework' technique.

After 1840 when Norwegians began to emigrate, in particular to America, the traditional white on white began to change with colour becoming evident. By the beginning of the 20th century, a lot of colour was to be seen with some pieces even having a mixture of several colours in the one piece.

Hardanger can still be worked in the traditional way. This is because of Norway's relative isolation which protected their work from outside influences and because over the past three centuries meticulous care has been taken in handing on the detailed techniques. Unlike other techniques such as English Ayrshire work and Danish Hedebo which came so close to being lost, the Hardanger technique was fortunate to survive the rapid changes of the Industrial Revolution through both the sharing of the technique and Norway's isolation. Today we are able to enjoy learning and working traditional and new forms of Hardanger to produce our own pieces for today and heirlooms for tomorrow.

Now we are looking at colour in a technique that until recently was mainly worked white on white or cream on cream. In this book, not only are we including colour, we are also including some stitches which are not evident in historical pieces of Hardanger. Thus we are expanding on the solid work given to us by those dedicated early embroiderers. The colours available today not only include plain colours but also variegated and hand dyed threads to say nothing about the wide choice in fabrics - to work on or to use as the background. All of which adds new dimensions to our chosen technique. As long as we have dedicated and interested embroiderers, all the old techniques will continue to be used and new ideas added. Use your imagination, share your ideas with others, pass on your techniques, but above all enjoy your hobby.

Before you Begin

Hardanger embroidery is fascinating. I enjoy all embroidery but Hardanger is my favourite and I hope this book will encourage you to become familiar with, and enjoy it, as much as I do.

In this section I cover a few basics which are useful to know including fabrics, threads and equipment to use. Tacking or basting is important. Please read this section carefully before beginning to stitch and refer back to it as required. Limited tacking is required in the Box tops, Mat and Christmas Runner but in the designs which are constructed more tacking is required and this is time very well spent.

The Stitches used in this technique are covered separately in the Stitch Section. We give large, clear, easy-to-follow diagrams with accompanying instructions. With these instructions and diagrams even if you have never stitched Hardanger before you will be amazed at how easy it is to learn the new stitches.

The Designs

The designs require increasing expertise as you work through the book. If you are new to the technique start with one of the first three designs to familiarize yourself with the techniques involved. Each design has full instructions, comprehensive charts and clear diagrams. They are shown in colour photographs and these may be used as an additional guide when stitching.

We give the number of threads used horizontally and vertically with each design (rounded up) so that if a different thread count is used you can work out the different amount of fabric required. Refer to the Thread section for different threads to use on different fabrics.

The filling stitches may be changed to suit your preference in each design, just refer back to the stitch section and make a personal selection.

Fabrics

There is a wide range of material available today. Most of the designs in this book are worked with fabric with 25 threads to the inch (25 count) or 28 threads to the inch (28 count). Do not hesitate to change the thread count to suit you as you need to enjoy working your embroidery and this can only be achieved by working on a material that you can personally see!

Other fabrics I have used for Hardanger fall into one of four categories:

Pure Linen	These range from Cork at 19 threads per inch (tpi), Montrose 28 tpi to Belfast 32tpi, or Edinborough at 35 tpi. Permin 28 tpi is the fabric I have chosen to use in many of the designs in this book.
Pure Cottons	These include the Oslo Hardanger fabric at 22 tpi and Linda at 27 tpi.
Cotton Viscose	These fabrics include Bellana at 20 tpi, and Lugana at 25 tpi also used in this book plus Brittney at 28 tpi and Murano at 30 tpi.
Cotton/Linen	This mix of natural fabrics includes Quaker at 28 tpi which I find a very useful fabric to work with and use often for Hardanger. I have also used other fabrics including Carrick at 45 tpi but would only recommend this if you feel in the need of a great challenge and wish to make a very delicate article!

Pure linens are enjoyable to use and launder well. A stain on a special piece of embroidered linen is generally able to be removed, whereas stains on fabric with a synthetic component can be difficult to remove. Any woven fabric that is an evenweave can be used for Hardanger, however do ensure that it has been dyed thoroughly. Surface dyeing is not satisfactory as it will show the white base colour on the ends that are cut which is not acceptable.

Threads

The threads most frequently used in Hardanger - Perle threads are easy to obtain and available in a good range of colours. They have a firm twist which helps to make them longer lasting and a sheen which looks most attractive. As a guide for choosing the correct weight of thread to go with your chosen fabric, for 25 count Lugana use Perle 5 for the kloster blocks and satin stitch and Perle 8 for the needle weaving, filling stitches, eyelets, cable stitch and buttonhole edging stitch if used. If a finer fabric is chosen, for example 28 count linen, use Perle 8 for the kloster blocks, satin stitch, etc and 12 for the needle weaving, filling stitches, eyelets. Similarly for a coarser fabric thicker weight threads will be necessary.

Occasionally, as in the handkerchief sachet which is stitched on 28 count linen, I used Perle 5 for some of the kloster blocks. In this case I wished to give extra emphasis to the stitching. Whilst I give these guidelines, remember they are just that, when stitching only you know the effect you wish to achieve.

Overdyed threads are also most attractive to use and work well in Hardanger. I have used Caron threads but if these are not available substitute a thread of a similar weight that is available at your local needlework store. When using Watercolours use one thread for 25 or 28 count linen for the kloster blocks etc and use Wildflowers for the needle weaving, filling stitches, and eyelets etc.

Remember, it can happen that some threads are not colour fast. Check this out. There are plenty to choose from so be selective and do not get caught with a thread that will cause you disappointment.

Needles

Most of the embroidery in this book is done on 28 count fabric yet you will find in some instances I recommend using #22 and #24 needles and other times #24 and #26 needles - this is entirely due to the variations in the threads used. Needle Sizes are given only as a guide - change size up or down according to what you are most comfortable with.
For me a Perle 5 thread works best with a Size 24 tapestry needle, but if this is difficult for you to thread, change to a Size 22 tapestry needle. I find Perle 8 and 12 work well in a Size 26 tapestry needle. Do not hesitate to experiment for yourself and remember the golden rule that a needle will wear out so do change to a new one if it becomes discoloured or stained or you feel the needle dragging through the fabric. The last thing you want is to damage your work. Sharp needles are used for construction.

Scissors

Fine, pointed and very sharp!

Embroidery Hoop

A 10 - 15cm (4-6") embroidery hoop is invaluable. It helps to open up the holes in the woven fabric thus making it easier to see as you work. It also helps to ensure your stitching is even.

Equipment

The usual sewing kit materials including the items already mentioned, plus a tape measure, pencil (sharp), pins and a pair of good tweezers which are an invaluable help in removing cut threads, especially in large designs.

Before you begin stitching

Neaten the Fabric

Woven fabrics can and do fray when they are handled. Neaten the raw edges of the linen by over sewing by hand or machine before you start to embroider the designs.

Tacking · basting

Tacking or basting is an invaluable tool in Hardanger embroidery. The initial tacking sets up the framework to work within and is time well spent. Tack using a fine tapestry needle, preferably #26 and sewing cotton in a strong contrasting colour.

I personally recommend that all tacking/basting is worked 'under four threads then over four threads'. The four threads are referred to as a 'group' this makes counting much easier as you count 'groups' not individual threads. Instructions in the designs also refer to 'groups'. Accurate tacking makes accurate stitching much easier and counting 'groups' rather than individual threads is much more convenient.

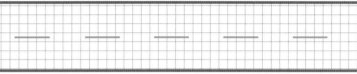
Tacking over and under four threads

When counting along a tacking line count each 'group' of four fabric threads as 'one' e.g.

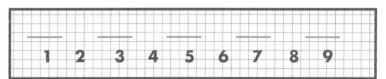

The amount of tacking required in the different designs does vary. Simple central tacking line/s are all that is required in the beginning designs, more is required in the constructed designs. Detailed tacking instructions are given with each design (where required) and as long as you follow these you will find stitching the designs is a joy!

Find the centre of the fabric

To find the centre of a piece of fabric fold it in half long ways and/or across ways depending on what is required and start tacking over and under 4-threads along the central fold.

When tacking lines are going to cross at the centre, make sure they cross one another so that there are 2-threads on each side of the cross. To do this, start the second line 2-threads from the centre but leave a long starting thread. Work from this point to the outside. Now rethread your needle at the centre and complete the remainder of the tacking line. In this way you get a little cross at the centre - the perfect guide for placement of satin stitch motifs if required. Avoid joining a tacking thread.

*Tacking at the centre
Note - 2 threads each
side of centre*

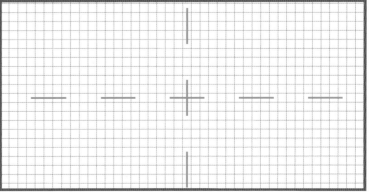

Use your tacking to check your stitching

When stitching keep checking your work against the accurate tacking so that any mistakes are quickly picked up and 'reverse stitching' is eliminated.

From the base of a kloster block, run an imaginary line with the back of your needle along the woven thread of the fabric from the kloster block to the matching point of a tacking thread. A quick check every so often in this way will let you know if all is well and help eliminate unnecessary unpicking and frustration at a later date.

Charts

On every chart in this book one line equals one thread.

Different stitches are shown in different colours - the actual thread used to stitch the different stitches may be the same.

For ease of stitching we have shown the charts for the designs as big as possible. Where a design is too large to be shown in one chart clear instructions and diagrams are given to ensure this is not a problem. There is **NO** overlap of one chart to another.

Signing and Dating your Work

Once you have completed the stitching do not forget to add your initials and the date. Sometimes this information can be incorporated in the design itself and so will be quite evident from the moment the project is completed. At other times it can be better not to include your details in the design, in these cases incorporate your initials inside the seams or hems. One day when the work is being carefully pulled apart, perhaps by a conservator, your identity will be revealed. Because the threads have been kept out of the light all those years the conservator will also be able to see the original colour of your thread, a nice touch.

Don't forget

Finally, before using or mounting your work, it should be carefully laundered. Just check that all your tacking threads have been removed before you place your embroidered piece into warm soapy water. Rinse thoroughly. Finally press your work while still damp from the wrong side on a well padded surface.

I hope you will have as much pleasure in stitching these designs as I had and remember, never hesitate to be prepared to change the colour of either fabric or thread to suit your own tastes and ideas.

Stitch diagrams

STARTING AND FINISHING

To Start

Waste knot
- Thread your needle then tie a knot at the end of the thread.
- About 5 or 6 cm (2") from where you will start working the first pattern, take your needle from the front (right side) to the back (wrong side).
- Bring your needle from the back up through the fabric at the point where you begin your first working stitch and stitch as required.
- On completion of stitching cut the knot off and finish the thread end following the instructions given with the different stitches

Back Stitch

Use this method for starting when working satin stitch motifs and buttonhole stitch.

Work a couple of little back stitches in an area that will later be covered by either the satin stitch or buttonhole stitch.

To Finish

Different finishing techniques are given with each stitch, however a good general instruction for finishing is to take your needle and thread to the wrong side of the work, change to a sharp needle and run the thread through the back of the completed work and cut off.

Bringing in a new thread

Instructions for doing this are given with each different stitching technique.

Kloster Blocks

Kloster Blocks are groups of five Satin Stitches worked over four fabric threads. They define the design and are a cornerstone 'stitch' of Hardanger Embroidery. Kloster blocks must completely outline any motif which is to be cut in preparation for filling stitches.

When working the Kloster Blocks do not pull the stitches too tight, they should lie neatly side by side.

As you work the kloster blocks, keep checking that you have:

(a) worked five satin stitches to a block

(b) not moved up or down a thread when changing the direction of a kloster block.

This is where you will find the tacking you carefully put in place before you began stitching so very helpful.

Needle/Thread

Kloster Blocks are always worked with thicker threads in larger needles than filling stitches.

Tips for Kloster Blocks

1. Always start and finish the thread at the end of a Kloster Block. Not only does this give strength to the threads prior to cutting them, it also ensures the 'join', especially when using variegated threads, is not so noticeable.

2. Kloster Blocks, along with tacking, are excellent checks for accuracy. If your Kloster Blocks do not align with your tacking, check for accuracy before continuing. Every now and then run an imaginary line with the back of your needle along the woven thread of the fabric from the base of the kloster block to the matching point of a tacking thread. A quick check like this will let you know if all is well and help eliminate unnecessary unpicking and frustration at a later date. If you don't have to unpick anything, count your blessings and then check again just to make sure!

3. Unlike some other types of needlework, it is acceptable to turn the work 90 degrees and continue working Kloster Blocks.

Do not proceed with filling stitches or cutting until all Kloster Blocks are in their correct place.

To Start

Pattern work in Hardanger usually commences with the working of kloster blocks. As there will be no stitching in which to hide your working thread, the only method to use at this stage is the 'waste knot' method (see page 11.)

Working in a Row, or Horizontally

Bring the needle up at the bottom of the stitch and go in four threads above.

Repeat until five satin stitches have been worked (fig 1).

When working kloster blocks in a row, work five satin stitches over four fabric threads then move to the next kloster block, four fabric threads further on. This will give a diagonal stitch on the wrong side of the work as shown.

Fig 1

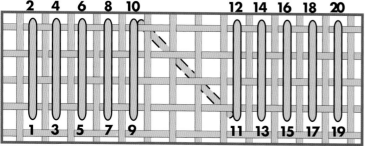

working horizontally

Working on the Diagonal

When working on the diagonal, kloster blocks are stitched at right angles to each other. Begin the first stitch of the second set of kloster blocks in the same hole as the last stitch of the first block (fig 2)

When working kloster blocks on the diagonal you must NEVER have diagonal stitches across the inner corners on the reverse side of the work as these could be cut accidentally at a later stage.

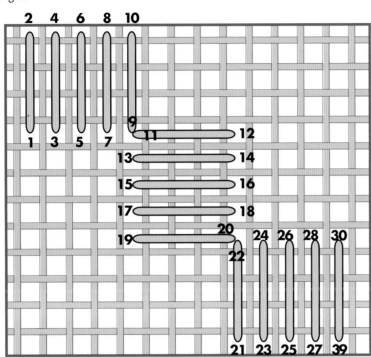

Fig 2

To finish

When you get to the end of the thread, take the needle to the back of the work and slip it back two or three kloster blocks, away from the last one worked, then weave to and fro three times through the back of a kloster block catching the first and last stitches at each turning. This will be nice and firm and look neater then taking the thread through the back of a whole row of blocks. Cut unused thread off neatly.

Joining a new thread

When starting a new thread in the middle of existing work there is now somewhere to 'hide' the start of the new thread. Take the thread under the last kloster block worked with the old thread, weave to and fro three times through the back of the kloster block again catching the first and last stitches at each turn. Bring the thread to the front of the fabric at the point where the pattern is to continue.

Counting Kloster Blocks

Through the designs you will find instructions to count, for example 'five kloster blocks'. Each group of five stitches is counted as 'one kloster block'.

Satin stitch

also known as Counted Satin Stitch, Geometric Satin Stitch

Satin Stitch motifs consist of straight stitches placed alongside each other. Favourite motifs in Hardanger include 'Stars', 'Ships', and 'Tulips'. The stitches should lie adjacent to each other without overlapping. Each stitch should lie flat on the fabric and should not 'pull' the threads of the fabric out of position.

Needle/Thread

Satin stitch is worked with thicker threads in larger needles than filling stitches and is usually worked using the same thread as for kloster blocks.

To Start

Satin stitch is usually worked in blocks and this makes it very easy to start - just work a couple of little back stitches in an area that will later be covered by the satin stitch (see page 11) and commence stitching the pattern as indicated.

Stitching the satin stitch motifs

When working a central motif, begin at the centre with a waste knot and work one area or sectiion of the motif first. When completed, take the working thread through to the back of the completed area and under the threads at the back down to the centre ready to work the second area. To complete, work round in a circle. When stitching motifs, bring the needle out of an empty hole and take it into a full or used hole. To work the last segment your needle will go in and out of a full hole. This is correct.

To Finish

Take your needle through to the back of your work, slip it under the stitching for a short distance, do a little slip knot (back stitch) and then take the needle under the stitching for a further distance.

Joining a new thread

Change the thread only at the end of a section, especially when working with variegated threads. Finish as above.

Tips

1. In order to keep the threads smooth and lying flat alongside each other, a laying tool may prove useful.

Fig 1

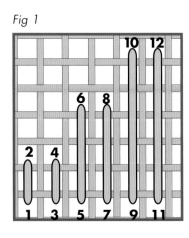

Buttonhole edging stitch

Blanket Stitch

This loop stitch is used to outline and enclose the edge of a design so that excess fabric can be cut away.

Needle/Thread

This is usually worked with a slightly finer needle and thread than has been used for the kloster blocks. For example if a Perle 8 has been used for the kloster blocks then I would recommend a Perle 12.

To Start

Secure thread using the back stitch method (see page 11). Bring the needle up at 1, down at 2, and up again at 3, looping the thread under the needle, as shown in fig 1. Continue working each new stitch one fabric thread to the right, with the needle down at 4 and up again at 5, fig 2.

Corners

When stitching an outside corner travel 'around' the corner, as in fig 2. All the stitches share the same fabric hole at the inner point and radiate out from here. The outside corners are worked differently in the various designs - detailed instructions are given with each design.

Note in this illustration one fabric thread either side of the corner stitch is not worked into.

When stitching an inner corner refer to fig 3. Again inner corners can be worked differently - check the instructions with each design.

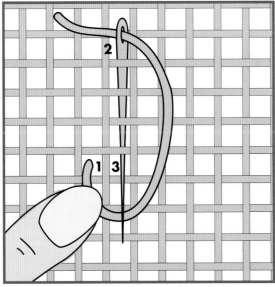

Fig 1

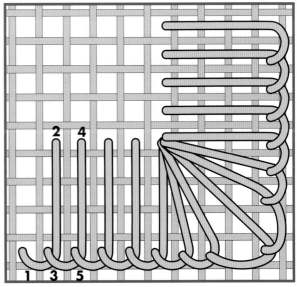

Fig 2

outer corner

15

To Finish

Take your needle through to the back of your work, slip it under the stitching for a short distance, do a little slip knot (back stitch) and then take the needle under the stitching for a further distance. Cut the thread end off neatly.

Fig 3

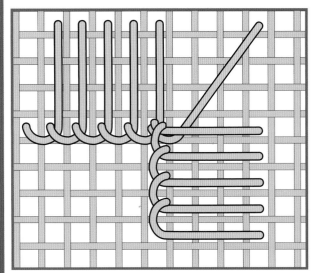

inner corner

Joining a new thread

It is important to make the join as seamless as possible and this is best done part way along a line, never at a corner. When the first thread is getting short put it to one side at the completion of a stitch, see fig 4.

Secure a new thread at the back of the work and bring it to the front one fabric thread further along, and continue as before. Return to the join and finish the old thread by taking the needle through the loop of the starting stitch worked with the new thread then down into the fabric four threads above. Finish thread neatly at the back fig 5.

Cutting threads at the Buttonhole Stitched Edge of a design.

All the Buttonhole Edge Stitch should be completed before any fabric is cut away.
Specific instructions for doing this are given with each design and they do vary.

Fig 4

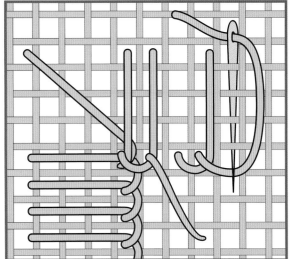

bringing in a new thread

Fig 5

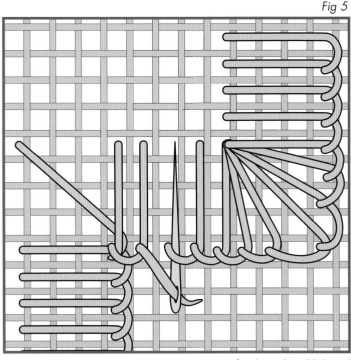

finishing the old thread

Tips

1. Take great care to stitch in every required fabric hole except when turning a corner. The loop may make seeing every fabric hole more difficult but as this stitch provides the finish for a raw edge it must be accurate.

2. Check regularly that the Buttonhole Edge Stitch is parallel to the Kloster Blocks where appropriate.

3. At regular intervals turn your work to the wrong side to check that you have not slipped up or down a thread while stitching.

Eyelets

Eyelets are not only decorative but also an attractive contrast to Kloster Blocks and Satin Stitch. The tension of the stitching must be firm *so the holes in the eyelets are all the same size.* Bring the needle up in the outer edge and take it down through the centre for all Eyelet stitches and variations. This enables you to pull the thread away from the centre. Eyelets can be worked over varying numbers of threads but in this book they are worked over two and three fabric threads. Three different eyelets are shown here.

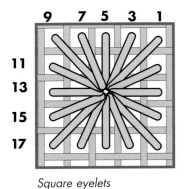

Square eyelets

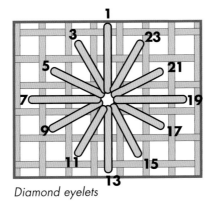

Diamond eyelets

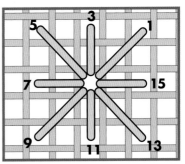

Algerian Eye stitch sometimes called Star Stitch

In the diagrams all even numbers are in the centre

Needle/Thread

Eyelets are worked with finer threads and needles than Kloster Blocks.

To start

If there is no other completed stitching in which to hide the working thread then use the waste knot method. Stitch following the charts always remembering to take the needle down in the centre.

To finish

On the wrong side of the work (preferably with a sharp needle) run the thread through the back of the completed work and cut off.

Joining a new thread

Never join a thread part way through working an eyelet.

Tips

1. When carrying thread from one Eyelet to another slip the working thread under the previously stitched area. This will avoid passing the thread directly across the opened centre "hole"- something that must never be done!

2. Keep the tension as even as possible in order to keep the stitches square and the open "hole" even.

17

Cable stitch
also known as Faggot stitch

This is a traditional pulled thread stitch which is also used extensively in Hardanger embroidery. It is frequently used for outlining the cut and filled diamond and triangle shapes found in the work. It can also be used for outlining satin stitch motif patterns. It gives an open lacey appearance when many rows are worked side by side. This adds another effective yet simple filling stitch to Hardanger. It is worked on the straight and on the diagonal and instructions are given for each.

Needle/Thread

Cable Stitch is worked with a finer needle and thread than is used for the kloster blocks, but is similar to that usually used for Buttonhole Edging Stitch.

Straight Cable Stitch

This stitch is worked over two fabric threads with the rows two threads apart as shown. Turn your material so that you are working down the fabric. Two rows, Row 1 and 2 are worked simultaneously. If another two rows are worked the stitches from Row 3 share the same holes as the stitches from Row 2.

To Start

Start with a waste knot (see page 11) then bring the needle up at 1 and work in the sequence shown until the charted length is reached.

To Finish

Take the working thread to the back of the work. Slip the needle and thread for a short distance through the completed stitching, work a slip knot (back stitch) then take the thread through a few more stitches before cutting off.

Joining a new thread

Threads can be woven in at the back of this stitch quite easily. Start as for finishing.

Corners

To turn a corner carefully follow the stitch sequence in the diagram. After working stitch '13-14' turn your work so that the point of the corner is at the top of your work and continue stitching as before.

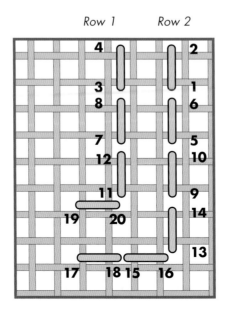

Double Cable Stitch - *worked on the diagonal*

This stitch is worked over two threads with the rows two threads apart.

To Start

Begin with a waste knot then bring the needle up at 1 and continue stitching in the sequence shown. Two rows, Row 1 and 2 are worked simultaneously. When working Rows 3 & 4 the stitches from Row 3 share the same holes as the stitches from Row 2. Work as shown for length required.

Finish and bring in new threads
as for Straight Cable stitch

Tips

1. Make sure the threads lie alongside, and not on top of each other.

2. If the stitch is pulled, make sure that the tension is even.

Fig 1   Single Cable Stitch

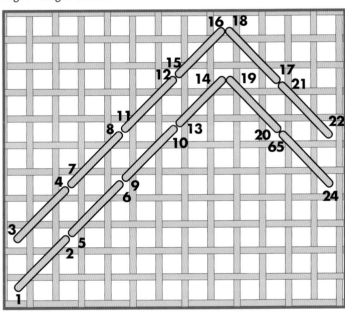

Fig 2   Double Cable Stitch

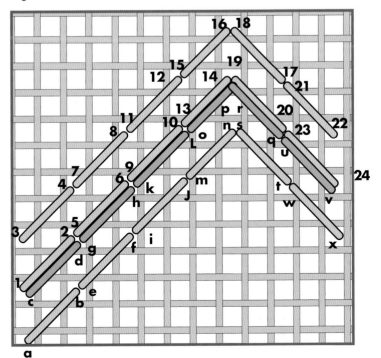

Cutting threads in preparation for fillings

Cutting threads in Hardanger is the section of work that beginners fear the most. Provided you have completed each step accurately and in the sequence given, then no cutting problems should arise. Remember the old refrain - count twice, check again, and cut once! Follow these simple guidelines and you will never cut an incorrect thread.

DO

- *Complete all surface stitching before cutting any threads.*
- *Use only very sharp, thin bladed scissors that cut well at the very tip.*
- *The threads to be cut must have a block directly opposite them, (see the threads marked with an 'x').*
- *The four threads that are to be cut, must have the five stitches of a kloster block surrounding them.*
- *Cut the same four fabric threads next to the kloster block at the opposite end of the cut area.*
- *Carefully remove cut threads with a pair of tweezers.*
- *Refer to the illustration showing the threads to be cut in a Hardanger design.*

DO NOT

- *Do NOT cut all the fabric threads in the whole design at the one time. When a large area requires cutting, work in small sections only. Cut an area which will fit comfortably into a small hoop (about 10-12cm, 4-5" in diameter) and complete the filling stitches before shifting the frame and cutting some more.*
- *Do NOT cut a thread on the long smooth side of a kloster block - see areas circled.*

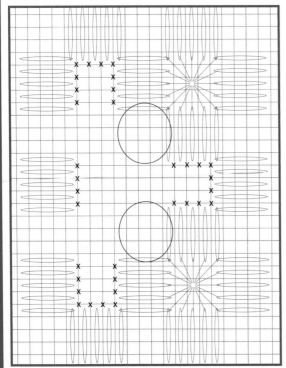

Cutting threads beside Satin Stitch

When one side is embroidered with the kloster block method and the opposite row is a solid row of satin stitch, cut the four kloster block threads and pull the cut threads back to the satin stitch row and from the wrong side, cut these four threads.

If you cut an incorrect thread

Do not despair! If an incorrect thread has been cut, all is not lost. Firstly remove the damaged thread then just replace this by withdrawing a thread from the outside edge of your piece of fabric and weave this back into the area where the damaged thread used to be!

Introduction to needle lace filling stitches

as used in Hardanger

useful information which applies to all needle lace filling stitches
- do read this before you begin

These are always worked with a finer needle and thread than those used for kloster blocks or satin stitch motifs. This section of work is completed once the threads of the woven fabric have been cut and pulled out leaving the four thread grid of the woven fabric ready for you to decorate with a choice of filling stitches. When working the fillings work within a small embroidery hoop of about 10-12cms diameter (4-5").

The filling is worked in a 'step' movement. On completion of the filling in the first bar move to the second bar to be filled - note the 'step' movement, see fig 1. When the bars to be stitched are adjacent to each other movement from one to the next is as shown. If the next bar to be stitched is not adjacent, but is separated for example, by a kloster block, take the working thread to the back of the work, thread it through the back of the kloster block before returning it to the front ready to continue your next bar.

All filling stitches, needle weaving and whipping are worked in stepped rows.
When a decorative filling is added, such as Dove's Eye's or Picots, these are usually worked in conjunction with your chosen filling of either weaving or whipping.

Fig 1 Numbering shows step movement for all filling stitches

Needle weaving

also known as Woven Bars

Needle weaving is worked after threads have been cut and removed leaving groups of four fabric threads that cross the cut area. These four fabric threads are woven together to form a bar.

Needle/Thread

Needle weaving is worked with finer needles and threads than kloster blocks.

To Start

Start with a waste knot see fig 1. Hold the working thread behind the four threads and bring it up to one side of the four threads. Start to weave by going over two fabric threads and down in the centre. Continue to weave under then over two fabric threads working in this 'Figure of Eight' movement as shown figs 1 & 2 changing the direction of the needle with each movement until the bar has been filled up. ***Do not pull too tightly as this may distort your embroidery.***

Fig 1

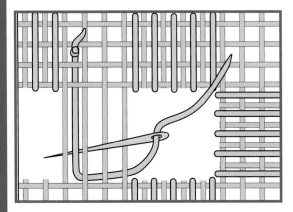

(It is important to start in this way so the needle is in the correct position when working picots and Dove's eyes.)

When the bar is completed, move to the next group of four threads in the 'step' movement. (To refresh yourself on the 'step' movement refer to fig 1 page 21)

To Finish

End an old thread on the wrong side of the needle weaving by taking the working thread through one side of a woven bar, turn, come back down the other side. Cut thread off.

Joining a new thread

Begin new threads at the beginning of a new bar using method given.

Fig 2

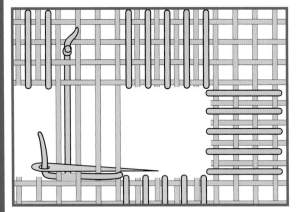

Tips

1. Keep tension consistent, in order to achieve even, firm needle weaving.

2. Stitching the same number of stitches on each bar helps achieve consistent tension, and helps retain the shape of the work.

Fig 3

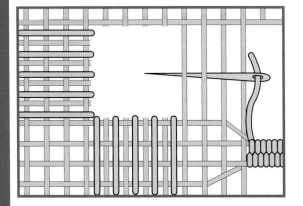

Over caste bars
also known as Wrapped Bars

In over caste bars the thread is wrapped round the four fabric threads that were exposed when the cut threads were withdrawn.

Needle/Thread
Stitched with finer needles and threads than kloster blocks.

To Start
Start with a waste knot (see page 11) then bring your needle to the front of the fabric at one end of the area to be filled. Working from left to right wrap the thread around all four fabric threads that were exposed when the cut threads were withdrawn.

When wrapping, the thread is pulled quite tight so that the fabric threads are drawn together. To make sure that the wrapped bars are smooth, each wrap must sit neatly next to the previous stitch, not on top of it.

To Finish
Weave the working thread into the back of the kloster blocks and use the kloster block method of finishing off, see page 13. To finish in the centre of a patterned area change to a sharp needle then pass the working thread through the back of completed wrapped bars before cutting thread end off.

Joining a new thread
Begin all new threads with a waste knot. Later, these can be threaded through completed worked areas.

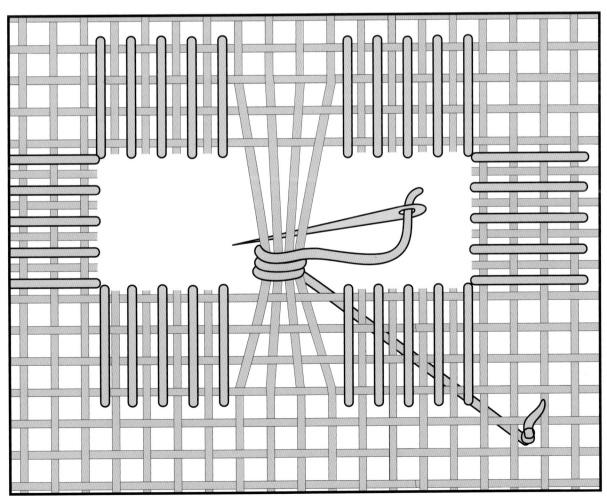

Woven bars with picots

A Picot is a French knot worked on the side of a needle woven bar. They are worked while the woven bar is being worked and give variety to woven bars.

To stitch

Picots are placed half way down the woven bar. They can be worked on both sides or just on one side of the bar. To make a picot, weave the bar in the usual way until the centre is reached, over 2-threads, under 2-threads. It is important to weave over 2-threads first.

Twist the thread once around the needle in an anti- clockwise direction, pull the thread firm around the needle, then place the point of the needle into the centre of the woven bar.

Push the twisted thread which is now firmly wrapped around the needle, up to the woven bar then place your forefinger under the fabric and your thumb on top over the needle and twisted thread as it goes through the woven bar. Still holding the fabric firmly pull the needle through and a picot will form. You can only feel this happen, not see it!

The picot will now sit neatly against the woven bar - if the picots should move to the back or lie on the top of the woven area, you could be working the needle weaving a little tightly.

To finish

Finish thread at the end of a working bar, never in the centre. Change to a sharp needle then pass the working thread through the back of one side of the woven bar, turn and come back down the other half of the same woven bar, then cut the thread end off.

Joining a new thread

As with needle weaving, only change thread at the end of a bar.

Tips

1. Over-vigorous pulling of the picots pulls them out of shape easily.

2. Practice makes picots sit more evenly, and even tension will help make picot knots a consistent size and shape.

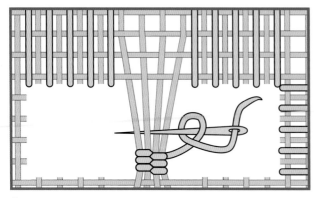

fig 1

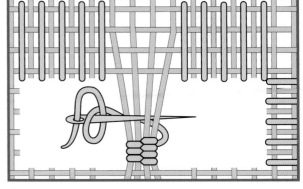

fig 2

Woven bars with Dove's eye filling

Dove's Eye Filling is a looped filling stitch which is used regularly in Hardanger embroidery. Each Dove's Eye filling is made up of four looped stitches, they are worked at the same time as the needle weaving of the bars in a design or if stitched in the centre of areas surrounded by kloster blocks, they are worked on completion of the kloster blocks.

Needle/Thread

Dove's Eye Filling is worked with fine needles and threads, similar to all other filling stitches.

To stitch Dove's Eyes when needle weaving

Needle weave three of the bars where the Dove's Eye is to be worked, then work to the centre of the fourth side, fig 1. If you have worked in a clockwise direction with the needle weaving, then the Dove's Eye will be worked in an anti-clockwise direction.

The Dove's eye is formed by working blanket stitch taking the needle down between the woven bars in the centre of each of the three completed woven bars. To complete the Dove's eye, and the trick that will ensure your dove's eye sits neatly, is to bring the needle *under* the first loop on its last journey before weaving the last half of the bar see fig 2.

To stitch Dove's Eyes into kloster blocks

The Dove's Eye is made up of the four looped stitches in the usual way. The only difference is each loop is worked under the central thread of the kloster block on the three sides. The fourth loop passes under the first loop to complete the Dove's Eye and is taken back into the kloster block fig 3.

Joining a new thread

As with needle weaving, only change thread at the end of a bar.

Tips

1. Practice will make your Dove's Eyes a regular shape.

2. Try to keep tension consistent, in order to keep Dove's Eyes identical.

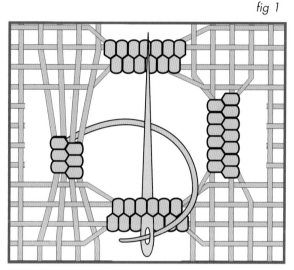

fig 1

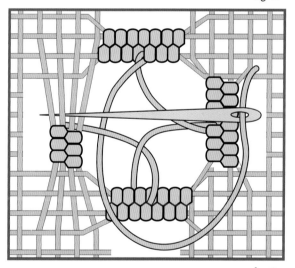

fig 2

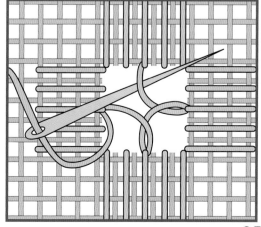

fig 3

Wrapped bars with Greek cross filling

Greek cross filling is an effective stitch which, when worked within an area, can give a pretty 'floral' effect.

Needle/Thread

Greek Cross Filling is worked with fine threads and fine needles, similar to other filling stitches.

To Start

Start with a waste knot. Begin by wrapping only two of the four threads in the bar in the area to be filled. Start working at the outer edge, ending at the centre point as in fig 1.

The Greek Cross effect is formed by needle weaving over two threads from the next group of threads and the wrapped bar just completed. Continue wrapping until the bar is stitched to half way. The effect to be achieved is for the wrapping to be firm and narrow at the centre but wider midway. At the midpoint continue wrapping down the bar until it is filled fig 3. Work on four sides until the bars are all worked.

Joining a new thread

As with needle weaving, try to change thread only at the end of a bar.

Fig 1

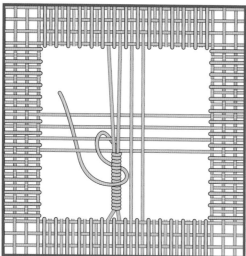

Fig 2

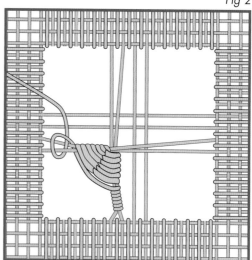

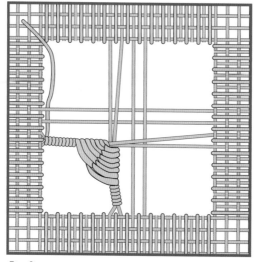

Fig 3

Oblique loop filling with twist

Oblique Loop Filling is an open lace-like filling stitch that can be used with whipped (overcast) or woven bars. It is worked after all four sides have been woven or wrapped continue using the same thread.

Needle/Thread

Oblique Loop Filling with a twist is worked with fine threads and a fine needle, similar to other filling stitches.

To Start

Start by weaving into the kloster blocks if you are at the beginning or by taking the thread through woven bars if part way through an area to be filled. Do use a sharp needle for this then change to the tapestry needle.

To Stitch

Bring the needle from the back to the front of the fabric at the centre of a corner at 1.
Take the thread across the open square and bring it up at 2, now take the needle around the first loop to create a twist as shown. This completes the first corner. Repeat at each of the four corners.
Do not forget to take the thread around the beginning of the first looped side to complete the first stitch.

To Finish

Take the working thread through to the back of a completed area, then take the thread up one section of the woven area and back down the second before cutting off the working thread.

Joining a new thread

Change thread only at the start of filling a new square.

Tips

1. Do not work oblique filling too firmly, try to keep your tension even.

Fig 1

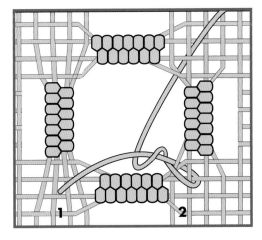

Fig 2

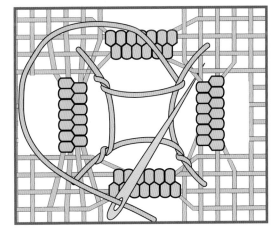

Antique Hem Stitch

This hem stitch is used to secure the hem of the the Christmas Runner. Stitch using a fine tapestry needle to avoid splitting the threads.

This stitch is worked from left to right. Hold your work with the folded edge of the hem against your body and the hem facing you. Bring the needle up two threads down from the folded edge of the hem, take the needle to the right pass it behind four threads of fabric at the edge of the hem (fig. 1). Next take the needle between the fabric and the hem (beside your first stitch) bring it through the hem two threads down as before (fig. 2). Continue in this way.

fig 1

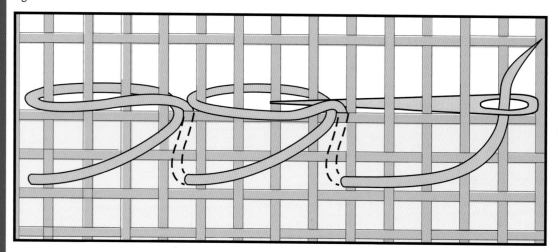

Shaded area
represents
the hem

fig 2

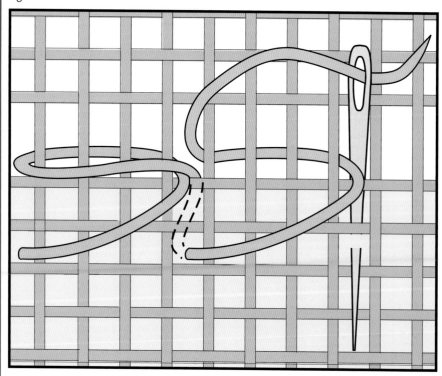

Mitre corners

Detailed instructions for tacking in preparation for working the hem and corners are given on page 50. Refer to these to prepare your fabric, which will look like fig 1 when the tacking is completed.

- With the tacking completed fold in one corner on the diagonal as shown on fig 2.
- Tack corner into position across the diagonal
- Cut away pointed corner, take care not to cut off to much. Do this for all four corners.
- Fold hem in at 'turn under' tack line
- Fold again at 'hem edge' tack line, line tacking up with tacked 'stitch line'.
- Tack hem, then sew in place with Antique hem stitch neatly slip stitching each corner together as you work.

fig 1

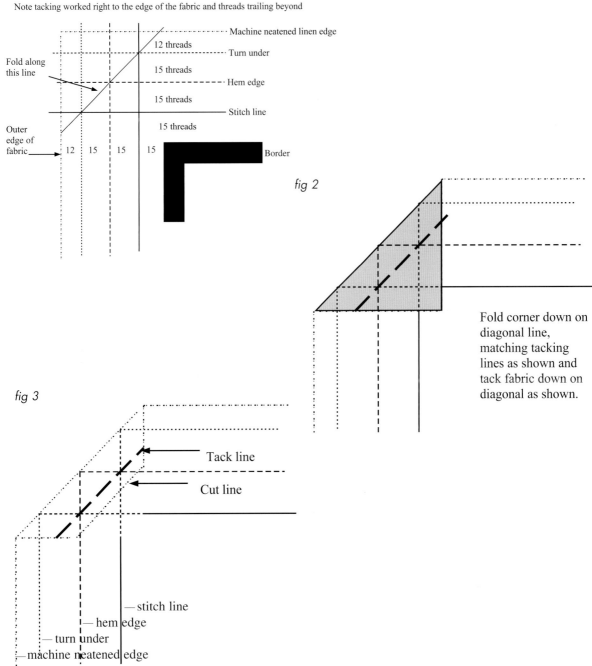

Note tacking worked right to the edge of the fabric and threads trailing beyond

Machine neatened linen edge
12 threads
Fold along this line — Turn under
15 threads
Hem edge
15 threads
Stitch line
15 threads
Outer edge of fabric
12 : 15 : 15 : 15 — Border

fig 2

Fold corner down on diagonal line, matching tacking lines as shown and tack fabric down on diagonal as shown.

fig 3

Tack line

Cut line

—stitch line
—hem edge
—turn under
—machine neatened edge

Hardanger Square Box

Hardanger Square Box

Boxes - we never have too many and a small box like this can have an infinite number of uses, especially for those easily misplaced small treasures. This little box top is an excellent introduction to Hardanger if this is a stitch technique that is new to you. Detailed instructions are given for its stitching to ensure that the end product is one you will be proud of.

Stitches used Kloster Blocks, Square Eyelets, Satin Stitch, Single and Double Cable Stitch, Needle Weaving.
Design size 130 threads wide and high

Requirements

Evenweave Fabric Cashel 28 threads per inch, Natural Colour 20cm sq (8"sq). This size fabric allows for about 4cm (1½") lacing on all sides.
Lining Fabric A piece of fabric to place under the completed embroidery to cover the padding - I used some more of the linen.
Padding A piece of lightweight dacron or something similar to be glued to the card before the embroidery is laced
Stiff card cut to fit the opening for the box
Threads   Caron Watercolours 'holiday' use one thread at all times
                 DMC Perle 8 #644 beige
                 Lacing thread
                 Contrasting sewing machine thread for tacking/basting.
Needles Tapestry #24 and #26, Sharp crewel needle No.7
Scissors fine and sharp pointed for use in embroidery, others for cutting card etc
Embroidery Hoop 10 - 12cm (4 - 5 inch)

Preparation

Machine neaten or hand stitch the outer edge of the fabric to prevent fraying (see Before you Begin page 9).
Find the centre of your square (easiest method is to fold the fabric in half, then half again and mark the centre with a pin).
Using sewing cotton in a #26 tapestry needle stitch vertical and horizontal tacking lines over and under 4-threads. At the centre, make sure the tacking threads cross one another so that there are 2-threads on each side of the cross This will make placement of the central satin stitch motif much easier. (For detailed information on tacking see page 9).

Accurate tacking makes it much easier to confirm accurate stitching. Hardanger, unlike some other forms of needlework, must be exact.

Handy Hint
For more information on starting, finishing and bringing in new threads refer back to the instructions with each stitch.

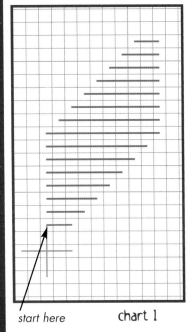

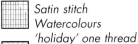 = tacking at centre of design

Note placement of first stitch in relation to tacking

each line on chart represents one thread

⊥ Indicates end of satin stitch

Satin stitch Watercolours 'holiday' one thread

Square eyelet p8#644

To Start

It is recommended that you stitch this design in the sequence given
Start stitching with the satin stitch motif at the centre (the tacking indicates the start point accurately see chart 1). This chart shows a small section of the central satin stitch motif, the complete satin stitch motif is shown on chart 2.

Start with a waste knot and bring the needle out in the correct position to work the central satin stitch motif using one strand of Watercolours 'holiday' and a #24 tapestry needle (See page 14 for more information on satin stitch).

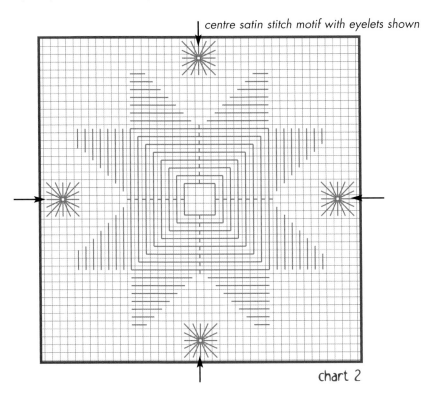

centre satin stitch motif with eyelets shown

chart 2

Still using one strand of Watercolours 'holiday' and a #24 tapestry needle work the two rows of kloster blocks. Start with a waste knot and stitch the inner row first. The second row is 12 threads out from the first. Remember each kloster block is composed of five satin stitches over four threads, refer to page 13 before you begin stitching to ensure you follow the correct stitch movement when changing direction.

Next work the cable stitch just beyond the central satin stitch motif then work the outer row of double cable stitch. Stitch using Perle 8 #644 and a #26 tapestry needle and start with a waste knot.

Still using the same needle and thread work the four eyelets. Each of these stands alone so starting and finishing neatly and securely is very important (see page 17).

Change back to a #24 needle and one strand of 'holiday' thread and work the outer satin stitch motifs.

With all the surface stitching completed you are ready to cut the threads where indicated by the zig zag line on the diagram. Refer to page 20 for more information on cutting threads.

Use Perle 8 #644 and a 26 tapestry needle to needle weave the threads left after cutting. Remember to start with a waste knot and bring the needle up to one side of the four threads and start weaving by going over two fabric threads and down in the centre. See page 22 for more information on needle weaving, starting, finishing and bringing in a new thread.

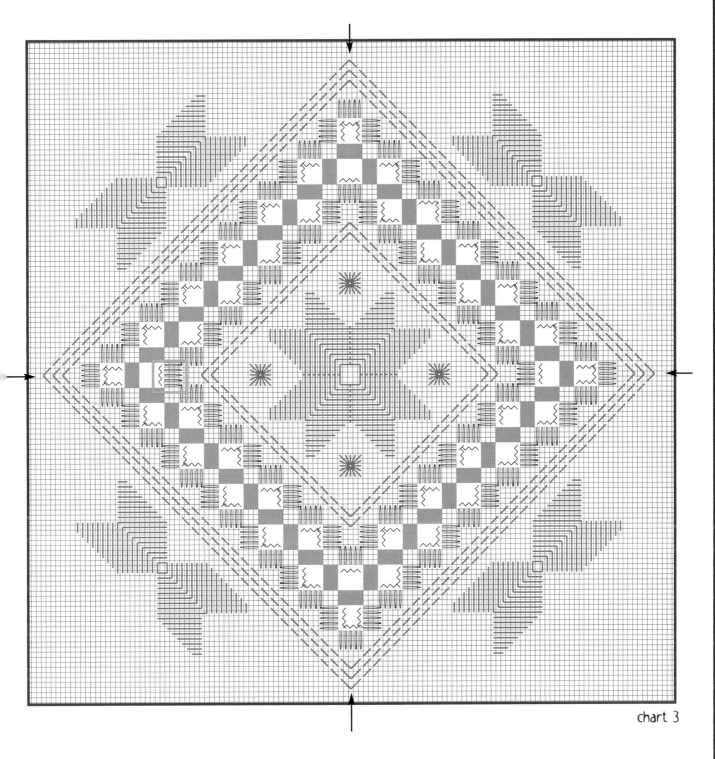

chart 3

KEY

Each line represents one thread

⊥ *Indicates end of each stitch in central satin stitch motif*

▢ *First kloster block worked here*

▨ *Cut threads here*

▥ *Satin stitch Watercolours 'holiday' one thread*

▥ *Kloster blocks Watercolours 'holiday' one thread*

▨ *Cable stitch P8 #644*

✳ *Square eyelet P8 #644*

▥ *Needle weaving P8 #644*

**When counting threads on a chart allow
4 - threads for each blank square
4 - threads for each needle woven bar**

33

To Complete

- Remove the tacking threads then carefully launder and press your embroidery.

- Cut card to fit the box lid, lightly glue dacron/padding to one side and leave to dry.

- Now cover the padded card with lining material by lacing it on smoothly. I used a piece of the embroidery linen.

- Centre the embroidered piece carefully over the lined card and lace smoothly into position, taking care that the line of the fabric threads exactly line up with the edges of the box lid and there is no distortion. Lace the embroidery to the card over the lining and padding.

- Place mounted embroidery in lid and enjoy your handwork.

This would also make a most attractive Christmas Ornament or a very useful coaster with added edging stitch.

Oblong Box

Oblong box top - Light Oak

Oak, a lovely light coloured timber, provides a most attractive background for a pretty piece of soft coloured fabric stitched in complimentary colours.

Stitches used Kloster Blocks, Satin Stitch, Square Eyelet, Woven Bars with Dove's Eye Filling
Design size width 220 threads x height 80 threads

Requirements

Evenweave Fabric Quaker 28 threads per inch, Zweigart 610, green 25 x 18 cm (10 x 7").
This size fabric allows for about 4cm (1¹/₂") lacing on all sides.
Lining Fabric a matching lightweight fabric is required to cover the padding on the card before the embroidery is laced over it. I used creamy yellow silk 18 x 25cm (7 x 10").
Threads   Caron Watercolours 'Pussy Willow' use one thread at all times

                DMC Perle 8 #739 cream
                Lacing thread
                Contrasting sewing machine thread for tacking/basting.
Needles Tapestry #22 and #24
Scissors fine and sharp pointed for use in embroidery, others for cutting card etc
Embroidery Hoop 10 - 12cm (4 - 5 inch)
Stiff card cut to fit the opening for the embroidered area
Padding to go between the embroidery and the card

Preparation

= tacking at centre of design

Note placement of first stitch in relation to tacking

each line on chart represents one thread

Machine neaten or hand stitch the outer edge of the fabric to prevent fraying (see Before you Begin page 9).
Find the centre of your square (easiest method is to fold the fabric in half, then half again and mark the centre with a pin).
Using sewing cotton stitch vertical and horizontal tacking lines over and under 4-threads. At the centre, make sure the tacking threads cross one another so that there are 2-threads on each side of the cross. This will make positioning the satin stitch motif in the centre of the design much easier. (for more information on tacking see page 9).

Accurate tacking makes it much easier to confirm accurate stitching. Hardanger, unlike some other forms of needlework, must be exact.

To Start

It is recommended that you stitch this design in the sequence given
Start stitching with the satin stitch motif at the centre (the tacking indicates the start point accurately see chart 1). This chart shows a small section of the central satin stitch motif, the complete satin stitch motif is shown on chart 2.

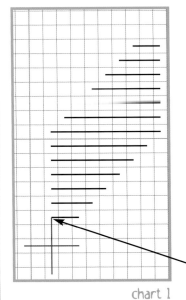

start here

chart 1

Start with a waste knot using one strand of Watercolours 'Pussy Willow' in a #22 needle and bring the needle out in the correct position to work the central satin stitch motif (see page 14 for more information on satin stitch). Complete all the satin stitch in the central design area.

Centre satin stitch motif

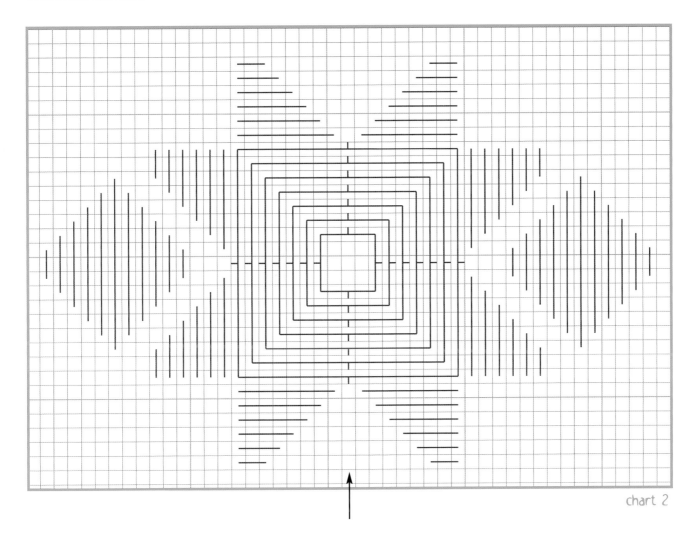

chart 2

each line on chart represents one thread

⊥ *Indicates end of each satin stitch*

Satin stitch Watercolours 'Pussy Willow' one thread

Still using the same needle and thread work the kloster blocks, again start with a waste knot. Stitch the inner row first. Remember each kloster block is composed of five satin stitches over four threads, refer to page 12 before you begin stitching to ensure you follow the correct stitch movement when changing direction.

Next work the cluster of Square Eyelets on either side of the centre satin stitch design. These are stitched with Perle 8 and a #24 tapestry needle. Start with a waste knot and finish the thread by weaving behind worked stitches on the back of your work.

Carefully cut the threads. Refer to page 20 for more information on cutting threads.

Use Perle 8 and a #24 tapestry needle to needle weave and form the Dove's eyes. Needle weaving strengthens the threads left after cutting and the Dove's eyes give an attractive lacy look to the design. Start with a waste knot and remember to bring the needle up to one side of the four threads and start weaving by going over two fabric threads and down in the centre. Refer to page 25 for needle weaving with Dove's eyes.

The Dove's eyes are not worked into each square so refer to the chart for the placement of these.

To Complete

- Remove the tacking threads.

- Carefully launder and press your embroidery.

- Cut card to fit the box lid, lightly glue dacron/padding to one side and leave to dry.

- Now cover the card with the lining material, lace it on smoothly.

- Centre the embroidered piece carefully over the lined card and lace smoothly into position, taking care that the line of the fabric threads exactly line up with the edges of the box lid and there is no distortion. Lace the embroidery to the card over the lining and padding.

- Place mounted embroidery in lid and enjoy your handwork.

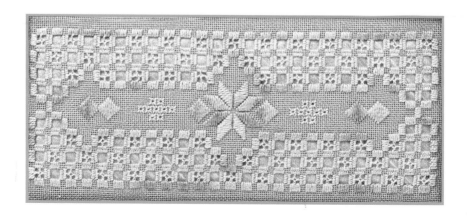

chart 3

each line on chart represents one thread

⊥ Indicates end of each stitch in central satin stitch

Satin stitch Watercolours 'Pussy Willow'

First Kloster block to be worked stitch inner row first

Kloster block Watercolours 'Pussy Willow'

Square Eyelets P8 #739

Needle weaving with Dove's Eyes - Perle 8 #739

Small Blue Mat

Blue Mat

This little mat looks very pretty with a vase of flowers or an attractive piece of china resting on it. When making if for yourself, choose fabric and threads that will match your décor. If you wish to make a gift for someone special, Antique white can be a very useful colour.

Stitches Used Kloster Blocks, Square Eyelets Buttonhole Edging Stitch, Satin Stitch, Woven Bars with Dove's Eye Filling
Design size width 200 threads x height 200 threads

Requirements

Evenweave Fabric Lugana 25 threads per inch Zweigart 501, Mid blue 30cm sq (12"sq)
Threads 1 skein Perle # 5 colour DMC 794 mid blue
            1 ball Perle # 8 colour DMC 794 mid blue
            tacking thread in a contrasting colour
Needles Tapestry 22 and #24
Embroidery Hoop 20cm (8 inch)
Scissors fine and sharp pointed

Preparation

Machine neaten or hand stitch the outer edge of the fabric to prevent fraying (see Before you Begin page 9). This is very important with Lugana as the fabric frays very quickly and easily.
Find the centre of your square (easiest method is to fold the fabric in half, then half again and mark the centre with a pin).
Using sewing cotton in a # 24 needle, stitch vertical and horizontal tacking lines over and under 4-threads. At the centre, make sure the tacking threads cross one another so that there are 2-threads on each side of the cross. This will make positioning the central satin stitch motif much easier. (See page 9 for more information on tacking)

Accurate tacking makes it much easier to confirm accurate stitching. Hardanger, unlike some other forms of needlework, must be exact.

To Start

It is recommended that you stitch this design in the sequence given
Start stitching beginning at the centre with the satin stitch motif (the tacking indicates the start point accurately (see chart 1). This chart shows a small section of the central satin stitch motif, the complete satin stitch motif is shown on chart 2.

Start with a waste knot, and work the central satin stitch motif using Perle #5 and a #22 tapestry needle. (See page 11 for more information on waste knots and page 14 for satin stitch).

+ = tacking at centre of design

note placement of first stitch in relation to tacking

each line on chart represents one thread

start here

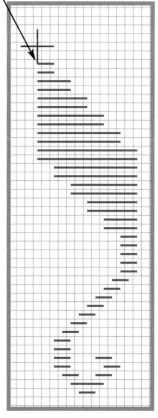

chart 1

chart 2

each line on chart represents one thread

⊥ *Indicates end of each satin stitch*

Satin stitch Perle 5 #794

Square Eyelets Perle 8 #794

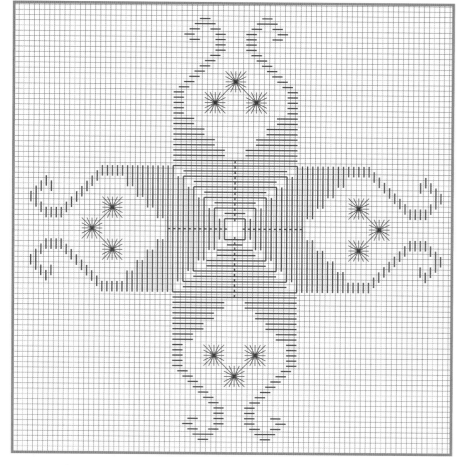

Now work all the kloster block patterns following chart 3 with Perle #5 and a #22 tapestry needle. Start with a waste knot and stitch the inner blocks first followed by those round the outside edge.

Remember each kloster block is composed of five satin stitches over four threads, refer to page 13 before you begin stitching to ensure you follow the correct stitch movement when changing direction. As you work the kloster blocks, keep checking that you have:

(a) worked five satin stitches to a block

(b) not moved up or down a thread when changing the direction of a kloster block.

This is where you will find the tacking you carefully put in place before you began stitching so very helpful.

Every now and then run an imaginary line with the back of your needle along the woven thread of the fabric from the base of the kloster block to the matching point of a tacking thread. A quick check every so often in this way will let you know if all is well and help eliminate unnecessary unpicking and frustration at a later date. If you don't have to unpick anything, count your blessings and then check again just to make sure!

A quarter of the chart is shown in chart 3. It is easy to work from this. Follow this quarter carefully, turn the chart at right angles and you will see the next quarter to stitch. A second method is to take four photo copies of the chart - match all four quarters together very carefully and then tape or glue them carefully together. This creates a complete chart should you find this easier to work from.

Next stitch the square eyelets (see page 17) using Perle #8 and a #24 tapestry needle. Begin working with a waste knot. When working the eyelets in the central satin stitch motifs start with the lower eyelet. Carry the thread to the next by taking the thread carefully behind the stitches worked on the just completed eyelet. Work the second eyelet from the base and you are in a good position to move to the third and final eyelet.

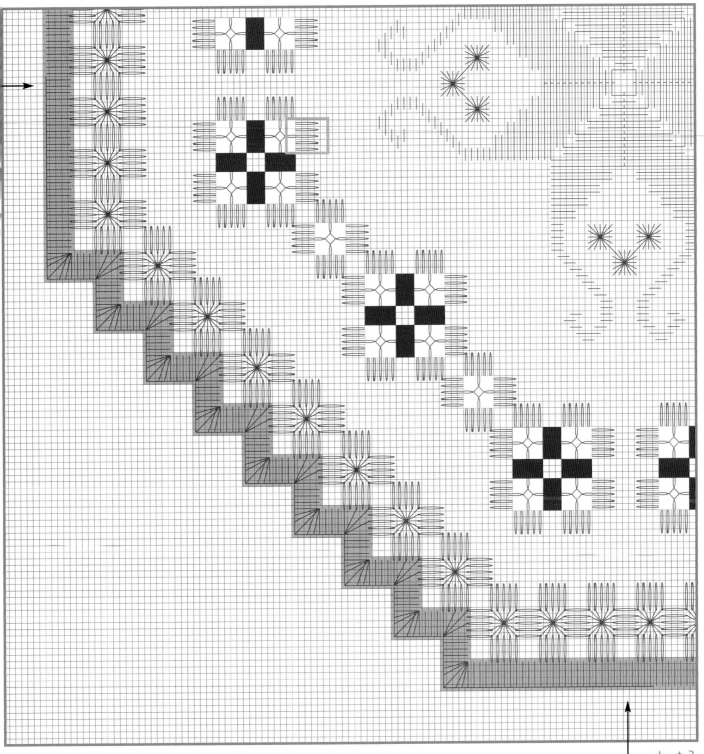

chart 3

each line on chart represents one thread

⊥	*Indicates end of each stitch in central satin stitch motif*
	Satin stitch Perle 5 #794
	First Kloster block to be worked here
	Kloster blocks Perle 5 #794
✳	*Square Eyelets P8 #794*
	Buttonhole edge stitch Perle 8 #794, note stitching at corners
	Needle weaving with Dove's Eye filling Perle 8 #794

43

When stitching the eyelets around the outer edge of the mat carry the thread from one eyelet to the next by slipping the working thread through the back of the kloster blocks.

The surface stitching is completed by working the buttonhole edge stitch (see page 15). Start with the back stitch method (page 11) and work round the outer edge following chart 3 using Perle #8 and a #24 tapestry needle.
Note The inner and outer corners are worked differently. At the inner corners buttonhole edge stitch is worked into every alternate fabric thread this means there are three stitches at each inner corner. At the outer corner buttonhole edge stitch is not worked into one thread on each side of the corner - this means there are only five working stitches around each outer corner. See chart 4.

Cut the threads carefully. Refer to page 20 for detailed information on cutting threads.

Use Perle #8 and a #24 tapestry needle to needle weave and form the Dove's eyes. Needle weaving strengthens the threads left after cutting and the Dove's eye filling gives a lacy look to the stitching.
Start with a waste knot. Remember to bring the needle up to one side of the four threads and start weaving by going over two fabric threads and down in the centre. Refer to page 25 for needle weaving with Dove's eyes.

To Complete

- Remove the tacking threads.

- To cut surplus fabric, leave one fabric thread next to the buttonhole edge stitch then cut the fabric away. (This avoids cutting the actual buttonhole stitch and when laundered the fabric shrinks slightly and all the 'ends' disappear!) Once completed, go round and cut away any small loose ends- these sometimes form at the corners.

- Launder your mat.

--- Enjoy ---

chart 4

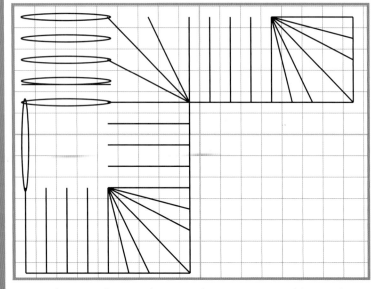

Note - there are three stitches at each inner corner and five stitches around each outer corner.

TIPS

1. When cutting threads turn your work to the wrong side. It is now easier to see each thread to be cut.

2. Cut one thread beyond the buttonhole edge stitch and cut just one thread at a time, for more information see page 55.

Christmas Runner

Christmas Runner

Carefully worked cloths such as this will become a treasured family heirloom. You will enjoy every stitch knowing that your family will take pleasure using it each year.

Stitches used Kloster Blocks, Satin Stitch, Square, Algerian and Diamond Eyelets, Needle Weaving, Antique hem stitch
Design size width 880 threads x height 180 threads

Requirements

Evenweave Fabric Brocade-Lugana 25 threads per inch, White with silver lurex 100cm x 50cm (40 x 20").
Threads   3 x DMC Perle 5 #699 Christmas Green
                1 x DMC Perle 8 #699 Christmas Green
                1 x DMC #80 Dentelles shade Blanc
                1 x DMC Metallise #5283 Silver (metallic thread)
                Contrasting coloured sewing cotton for tacking thread
Needles Tapestry #22, #24 and #26
Scissors fine, pointed and very sharp
Embroidery Hoop 10 - 12cm (4 - 5 inch)

Preparation

Machine neaten or hand stitch the outer edge of the fabric to prevent fraying (see Before you Begin page 9). This is very important with Lugana as the fabric frays very quickly and easily.

Find the centre of the fabric (easiest method is to fold the fabric in half length ways and tack over and under 4-threads using contrasting sewing cotton and a #26 tapestry needle then fold the fabric in half widthways and tack). All tacking is over four threads and under four threads. The four threads are referred to as a 'group' this makes counting much easier as you count 'groups' not individual threads At the centre, make sure the tacking threads cross one another so that there are 2-threads on each side of the cross (see page 9). This will make positioning the satin stitch motif in the centre of the mat easier.

each line on chart represents one thread

 Algerian Eyelet Perle 8 #699 & one strand of silver thread

 Satin stitch Perle 5 #699

Accurate tacking makes it much easier to confirm accurate stitching. Hardanger, unlike some other forms of needlework, must be exact.

To Start

It is recommended that you stitch this design in the sequence given
Begin with the satin stitch stars at the centre, carefully following chart 1 which shows the central star only. Stitch using a #22 tapestry needle and Perle 5 #699 and start with the back stitch method page 11. Turn to Chart 2 and using the tacking lines as a guide stitch the three stars across the centre first. Do not carry the thread between stars, stitch each star, finish the thread then start the new star. Count out from the centre star for the placement of the remaining stars.

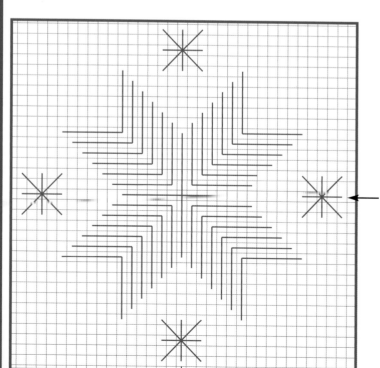

chart 1

Next stitch the four Algerian eyelet stitches which are worked around each of the satin stitch stars at the centre. These are stitched in a #24 tapestry needle using Perle 8 #699 and one strand of silver thread in the needle, stitched as one. To start secure the thread by taking a small back stitch in the back of the worked satin stitch stars and on completion of each star carry the thread through the back of the satin stitch to the starting position for the next Algerian eye. Finish the threads in the back of the satin stitch stars.

Chart 2 shows the Diamond Eyelet at the top of the first Christmas tree. This Diamond Eyelet is repeated on Chart 3 where the whole tree is shown with the diamond eyelet at the top.

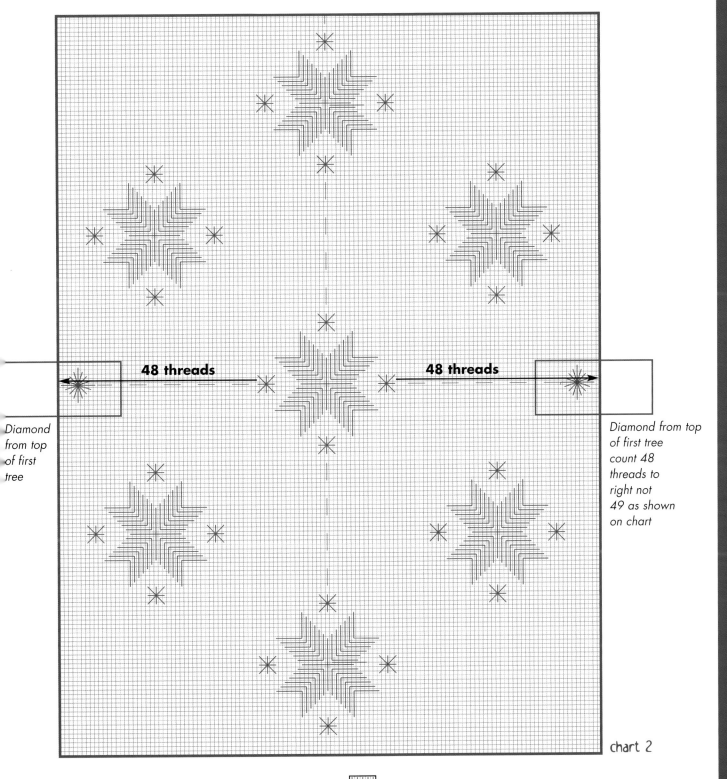

48 threads

48 threads

Diamond from top of first tree

Diamond from top of first tree count 48 threads to right not 49 as shown on chart

chart 2

each line on chart represents one thread

 Satin stitch - Perle 5 #699

 Algerian Eyelet - Perle 8 #699 & one strand of silver thread

 Diamond Eyelet one strand of silver thread

Working from the centre star, count to the left and right 12 groups (48 fabric threads - it is actually 11 whole groups with a half group top and bottom!) from the base of the Algerian eyelet in the centre of the design, see arrows Chart 2, Page 47. This brings you to the top in the centre of the kloster block pattern which forms the tree. The diamond eyelet is shown on the chart but is not stitched till later. Follow the chart carefully .

Remember each kloster block is composed of five satin stitches over four threads, refer to page 13 before you begin stitching to ensure you follow the correct stitch movement when changing direction. To position the second Christmas tree count down 10½ groups (42 threads) from the base of the trunk of the first tree. This brings you to the top of the centre stitch in the kloster block at the top of the tree.

Note that the top kloster block of each tree is stitched with the threads forming a point and the trunk of each tree is formed by three kloster blocks - refer to the chart.

The square eyelets around the edge of each tree and the diamond eyelets resting on the 'boughs' of the tree are worked next using silver thread in a #26 tapestry needle. One thread is used for working both the square eyelets and diamond eyelets.

chart 3

With the surface stitching completed it is time to cut the threads ready for needle weaving. Refer to page 20 for more information on cutting threads.

Use Perle #8 and a #26 tapestry needle to needle weave the threads left after cutting. Remember to start with a waste knot and bring the needle up to one side of the four threads. Start weaving by going over two fabric threads and down in the centre. See page 22 for more information on needle weaving, starting, finishing and bringing in a new thread.

Placement of the kloster block border

For the correct placement of the kloster block border count down the lengthways central tacking line 41 'groups' (164 threads) from the base of the second Christmas tree. Chart 4 shows the placement of the border in relation to the central tacked line, and half of the narrow edge border with one corner. The repeat for the long edge is shown on the chart.

Using Perle #5 699 start at one of the tacked centre lines with a waste knot and work the kloster block edging. As always the tacked lines are a very handy check that you are stitching correctly. To check, run the blunt end of a needle along the fabric from the kloster blocks back to the centre tacked line to ensure the kloster blocks are starting and finishing at the right places!

On completion of the kloster block border work the square eyelets in each corner using one strand of silver thread in a #26 needle. Start and finish the thread in the back of the kloster blocks.

KEY - Chart 3

each line on chart represents one thread

 Kloster blocks - Perle 5 #699

 Diamond eyelets - one strand of silver thread

 Square eyelets - one strand of silver thread

 Needleweave - Perle 8 #699

KEY - Chart 4

each line on chart represents one thread

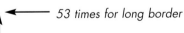
Repeat from ← 53 times for long border

Count out 41 'groups' (164 threads) from the base of the second Christmas tree to start the Kloster block border

 Kloster blocks - Perle 5 #699

 Square eyelets - one strand of silver thread

This chart shows one half of the narrow edge border

chart 4

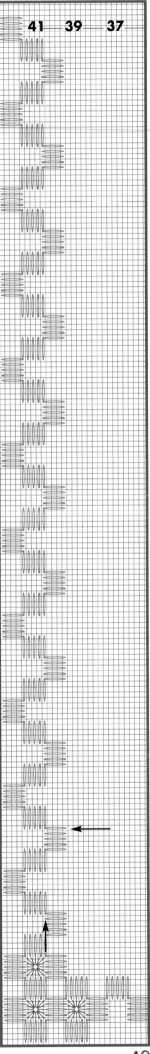

To Complete

- From the outer edge of the kloster blocks, count out 15 fabric threads. With a #26 tapestry needle and contrasting tacking thread, run a tack line down the length of your fabric.

- From this tack line count out 15 fabric threads. Run a second tack line parallel to the first.

- From the second tack line, count out 15 fabric threads and run a third tack line.

- Repeat this on the other three sides. At the corners the tack lines will cross one another. This is correct.

- On all four sides count out a further 12 threads. Withdraw the thirteenth thread. Cut surplus fabric away along the lines of the withdrawn threads. Neaten the four cut edges. Mitre corners following the instructions on page 29. Fold hem along each tack line, tack in place. Sew the hem with Antique hem stitch page 28 using Dentelles 80 white and a #26 tapestry needle. As you are not withdrawing any threads in which to stitch you achieve a very fine pin hole appearance - hence this stitch is sometimes called 'pin' stitch.

-- Place this with pride on your table at Christmas --

Handkerchief Sachet

Handkerchief Sachet

It is nice to have pretty things in one's home and this Handkerchief Sachet would look attractive in a drawer or on top of a dresser. Put it in the bathroom with paper tissues in it for guests or in the guest room ready for visitors - what could be more welcoming.

Stitches used Kloster Blocks, Square, Diamond and Algerian Eyelets, Satin Stitch, Needle Weaving with Picots, Buttonhole Edge Stitch
Design size width 440 threads x height 160 threads

Requirements

Evenweave Fabric Quaker 28 threads per inch, 'Rue Green' 718, 45cm x 20cm (18$\frac{1}{2}$ x 8")
Thread 1 ball DMC Perle 8 #928 grey green
1 ball DMC Perle 12 #928 grey green
1 skein DMC Perle 5 #819 pale pink
1 skein DMC Perle 8 #819 pale pink
1 skein Caron Watercolours 'Seashell' use one thread at all times
1 skein Caron Wildflowers 'Seashell'
Contrasting sewing cotton for tacking
Matching sewing thread
Needles Tapestry #24 and #26
Embroidery Hoop 10 – 12cm   (4 to 5 inch)
Scissors fine, pointed and very sharp

Preparation

Neaten the outer edge of the fabric to prevent fraying (see Before you Begin page 9). Fold the fabric in half lengthways and using contrasting sewing cotton tack over and under 4-threads with tacking thread and a #26 tapestry needle for the length of the fabric.

To Start

On the narrow edge, measure 2.5cm (1") down the tack line and centre the first kloster block (clearly marked on chart 1) over the tacked line, start with a waste knot. Follow the chart to work the outer kloster blocks with Perle 8 #819 and a #26 tapestry needle. In this design the outer kloster blocks are worked with Perle 8 but the kloster blocks surrounding the satin stitch design at the centre and shown in green are worked with a slightly heavier weight of the same thread, Perle 5 #819. This makes the kloster blocks more prominent.

Remember each kloster block is composed of five satin stitches over four threads, refer to page 12 to check out how to start, finish, bring in a new thread and to ensure you know the correct stitch movement when changing direction. At the side of the design (adjacent to the cut areas) satin stitch is worked between two areas of kloster blocks. It is also worked around the corners between the kloster blocks on the outer edge - this is worked using the same thread (Perle 8) as the outer kloster blocks and can be worked at the same time.

Satin stitch Perle 8
#928
grey green

chart 1

each line on chart represents one thread

Half of design shown, black arrows indicate centre

⊥ Indicates end of each satin stitch

☐ Start kloster blocks here

▥ Kloster blocks blue worked in Perle 8 #819

▥ Kloster blocks green worked in Perle 5 #819

▤ Satin stitch at side of design between Kloster blocks - Perle 8 #819

→ Start buttonhole edge stitch here

▨ Note - worked over 2 threads Wildflowers 'seashell' for flap and Perle 12 #928 used for rest of sachet

▥ Satin stitch, 3 motifs Watercolours 'seashell'

✳ Algerian eyelets Wildflowers 'seashell'

✳ Diamond eyelets Perle 12 #928

✳ Square eyelets Perle 12 #928

▦ Needleweaving with Picots Wildflowers 'seashell'

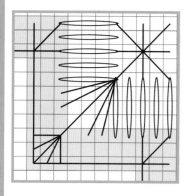

Complete the outer edge by working buttonhole edge stitch over TWO fabric threads only. Use Wildflowers 'seashell' and a #26 tapestry needle. Following the graph take care to turn on the inner and outer corners correctly, as shown.

Begin with a waste knot at the point shown on the graph by the pink arrow. Finish at the same point on the opposite side as the rest of the buttonhole edge stitch is worked using Perle 12 #928 (grey green).

Work the central satin stitch motif. Start with a waste knot and stitch using Watercolours 'Seashell' and a #24 tapestry needle. To complete the central design change to Perle 12 #928 (grey green) and work the square and diamond eyelets. Start and finish the threads in the back of the satin stitch motif.

With Wildflowers 'seashell' and a #26 tapestry needle, work Algerian eyelets into the centre of each kloster block around the outside edge and in the area between the two rows of satin stitch at the top of each side.

Whilst the flap is outlined with Kloster blocks and satin stitch in Perle 8 #819 and buttonhole edging stitch using Watercolours 'seashell', the bag section is stitched using grey green Perle 8 and 12. To form the bag section of the sachet, start by working satin stitch over four fabric threads, four threads above the top kloster blocks. Use Perle 8 #928 (grey green) with a #26 tapestry needle and begin with a waste knot. Turn the corner at the point shown on the chart, taking care to work as shown. This stitching is worked round all four sides and is the same width as the front of the sachet and 26.5cm (10½") in length.

Buttonhole edge stitch is worked outside the satin stitch over TWO threads only using Perle 12 #928 (grey green) and a #26 tapestry needle. Begin stitching from the point where the Wildflowers 'seashell' finished. Work around the three sides finishing back at the point where the Wildflowers 'seashell' commenced.

To complete the embroidery on the sachet, two small motifs are worked each side of the front at the base of the bag. Find the centre of the 26.5cm (10½") length. From this centre line and the outer buttonhole stitch edge measure in 3cm (1¼") and position the small motifs here, see chart 2. Each motif is worked with Watercolours 'seashell' with a #24 tapestry needle. Eyelets are worked with Perle 12 #928 (grey green) and with a #26 tapestry needle.

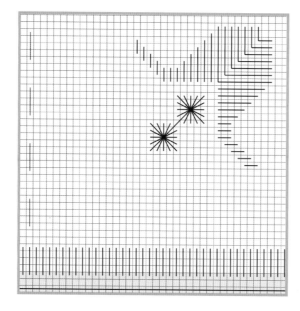

chart 2

each line on chart represents one thread

Satin stitch motif Watercolours 'seashell'

Square eyelets - Perle 12 #928 grey green

Satin stitch worked at edge over 4 threads using Perle 8 #928 grey green

Buttonhole edge stitch worked over 2 threads - Perle 12 #928 grey green

Cutting for Needle weaving

Refer to page 20

In this design there is a row of satin stitch opposite blocks of kloster blocks. It is an advantage to cut first the threads of the inner kloster blocks. Pull back the cut threads to the row of satin stitch. Turn the work to the wrong side and cut each hanging thread close to the satin stitch. Now complete cutting in the usual way.

Needle weaving

Work your chosen filling stitch with Wildflowers 'seashell' and a #26 tapestry needle. I used needle weaving adding picots in the central area - refer to chart for placement of the picots. See page 24 for needle weaving with picots. You could use Dove's eyes if you prefer. Whatever your choice of filling - choose what you like to stitch - it is so important that you enjoy your work.

To complete

- Along the two long sides and the straight end, remove the thread adjacent to the buttonhole edge stitch - that is the first thread beyond the buttonhole edge stitch. From the wrong side cautiously cut away the surplus fabric along the line left by the withdrawn thread. Withdrawing a thread helps to prevent damaging your embroidery and allows for a good clean cut.

- Around the shaped end of the sachet, leave one fabric thread adjacent to the buttonhole edge stitch and cut away the fabric between this fabric thread and the next. When the cutting has been completed, there will be two small threads left hanging at each inner corner. Carefully cut away.

- Fold the straight end of the embroidery up to the satin stitch border running across the embroidery. Line up the two rows of satin stitch. Join the sachet together by working a running or tacking stitch between the buttonhole edge and the satin stitch. Work over two threads using a matching sewing thread and a #26 tapestry needle. Begin stitching at the top, once at the base, stitch back up to fill the spaces left on the way down. The end result is a smooth line which looks the same on both sides. It is preferable to use the one length of thread for both journeys.

- Launder your sachet and then you are finished!

--- Enjoy ---

Cutting off surplus fabric
There are two different methods used at different times.

- *When cutting a **stepped** buttonhole edge leave **one** fabric thread **adjacent to the buttonhole edge stitching** and cut away the fabric between this fabric thread and the next. There is NO withdrawn thread to guide the cutting. There will be two small threads left attached at each inner corner, cut these away later once all the stepped cutting has been completed.*

- *When there is a long straight line of buttonhole edge stitching with no corners or steps remove the thread NEXT to the buttonhole edge stitch and from the wrong side of your work, cut away the surplus along this withdrawn thread line.*

Sometimes just one of these methods is used, other times both are required.

Travelling Hussif & Accessories

Travelling Hussif & Accessories

I have created and given to each of my four daughters one of these hussifs as a special gift when they left home. The first was made over 20 years ago and I am now being reminded that age is taking its toll and that only 'Mum' can replace such a well loved and used article. The wonderfully colourful array of fabrics and threads now available make this hussif a joy to create.

Stitches Used Kloster Blocks, Satin Stitch, Square Eyelets, Diamond Eyelets, Buttonhole Edging Stitch, Diagonal Cable Stitch, Needle weaving

Design size width 430 threads x height 180 threads - hussif case balance of width of fabric used for self lining

Requirements

Evenweave Fabric Permin 'Desert Sand' 28 threads per inch, fat quarter 70 x 50cm (28 x 20")
Threads   2 x Perle 5 DMC 3685 'mulled wine'
Perle 8 DMC 3685 'mulled wine'
Wildflowers by Caron 'Royal Jewels'
tacking thread in a contrasting colour
sewing thread to match background fabric
Small piece of iron-on interfacing for the scissor holder
Small piece of leather approximately 5 x 2.5cm (2 x1")
Wool flannel for the needle case, approx. 10 x 20 cm (4 x 8")
Lightweight batting approx. 10 x 20 cm (4 x 8")
Pencil HB   sharp
Pins A packet of pearl headed pins
Needles   Tapestry #24 and #26 and a fine Sharp
Embroidery Hoop   10 - 12cm (4-5")
Scissors fine, pointed and very sharp

NOTE *The instructions given here are for the fabric specified, if fabric with a different thread count is used metric and imperial measurements will need to be adjusted.*

Preparation

Machine neaten or hand stitch the outer edge of the fabric to prevent fraying (see Before you Begin page 9).

All tacking is under and over four threads. **The four threads are referred to as a group' this makes counting much easier as you count 'groups' not individual threads. In this design the vertical tacking needs to start from the same point as one end of the horizontal tacking, see chart 1. As you tack check from time to time that the stitches line up with each other as shown. As this design is 'constructed' extra tacking is required. Accurate tacking makes it much easier to confirm accurate stitching. Hardanger, unlike some other forms of needlework, must be exact. For more information on tacking see page 9.**

chart 1

Refer to the layout diagram for placement of the various items in the set. There are four separate parts to the Traveller's Hussif, The Hussif or Case, Needle book, Pin holder and Scissors holder. The Hussif is placed along the 70cm (28″) length edge of the fabric and the other three items fit beneath. The other items are shown with the approximate amount of fabric they require given in centimetres and inches (a generous allowance has been made) and on the Case and Needlebook further numbers are shown in circles these are the number of 'groups' of four tacked threads along each side of the item. Do not cut pieces of the set out until all the embroidery is completed, it is much easier to use the hoop and you will not lose pieces of fabric!

The Hussif and Accessories Layout Diagram

Selvedge Edge ——▶

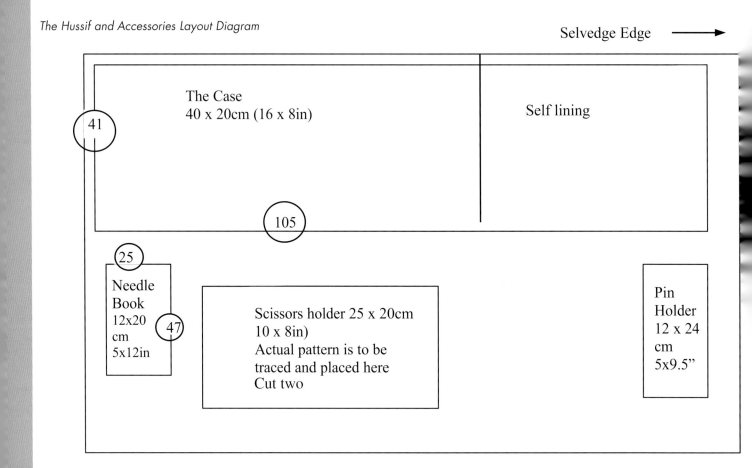

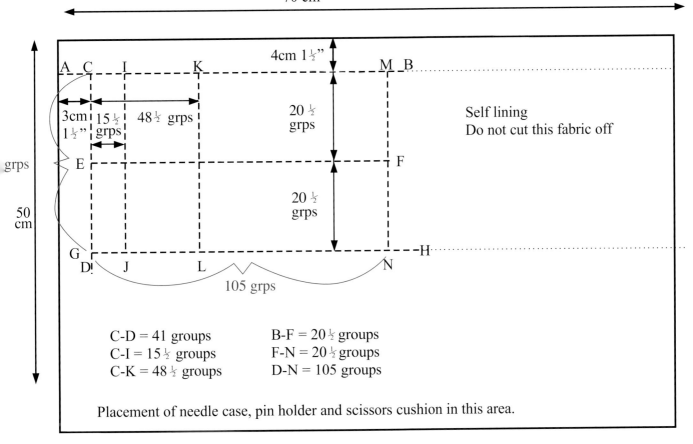

70 cm

50 cm

4cm 1½"

20½ grps

20½ grps

Self lining
Do not cut this fabric off

grps

3cm 1½" 15½ grps 48½ grps

105 grps

C-D = 41 groups
C-I = 15½ groups
C-K = 48½ groups

B-F = 20½ groups
F-N = 20½ groups
D-N = 105 groups

Placement of needle case, pin holder and scissors cushion in this area.

Line AB Along one side of the 70cm (28") edge, measure down 4 cm (1½"). With contrasting tacking thread in a #26 tapestry needle, run a tack-line over and under four threads across the fabric for approximately 40cm (16"). Start at the left hand edge. This is line A-B which is the top edge of the Hussif. The remaining length of material does not need to be tacked as it is the lining and is not embroidered. Do not cut off.

Line CD Measure 3cm (1½") to the right along line AB and run tack line CD 41 'groups' down from this point making sure this line begins at the start or finish of a 4-thread group on Line AB. This is line CD.

Line EF From tack line AB, count 20½ 'groups' down line CD and run tack line EF parallel to line AB. Make sure each 4-thread group lines up exactly to the corresponding group on line AB. This line marks the centre of the hussif.

Line GH From tack line EF, count 20½ groups down line CD and run tack line GH. This is the lower outside edge of the case. Again make sure each 4-thread group lines up exactly to the corresponding group on line EF.

Line IJ From tack line CD count to the right along tack line AB 15½" 'groups'. Run tack line parallel to CD. This line I J gives the position of the satin stitch design for the front flap.

Line KL From tack line CD count to the right along tack line AB 48½ 'groups' and run tack line KL. This gives the position for the satin stitch design on the back of the Hussif.

Line MN From tack line CD count to the right along line tack AB 105 'groups' and run a tack line parallel to CD. This is the right hand end of the hussif. The material beyond this tack line will be folded in to form the lining.

Handy Hint
Run blunt end of needle down linen between lines of tacking as you are working to check the tacking groups are starting and finishing at the same threads

59

Each line on chart represents one thread

⊥ *Indicates end of each satin stitch*

+ *Indicates centre*

Satin stitch Perle 5 #3685

Square eyelet - centre Wildflowers 'Royal Jewel'. Not shown on chart to make placement of first satin stitch easier

Diamond eyelets Wildflowers 'Royal Jewel'

To Start

Satin Stitch Motifs

Start stitching by working the first of the two satin stitch designs, the one on the flap of the Case is positioned where the line I-J intersects the line E-F. Begin with a waste knot and using Perle 5 #3685 in a #24 tapestry needle stitch following chart 2. Stitch the second satin stitch motif where the line K-L intersects the line E-F. Use the tacking lines to centre both motifs.

Kloster Blocks

Next start stitching the kloster blocks. Remember each kloster block is composed of five satin stitches over four threads, refer to page 13 before you begin stitching to ensure you follow the correct stitch movement when changing direction.

There are two main areas of kloster blocks - those worked round the edge of the Case and those worked in the central panel. The kloster blocks in the central panel are worked first. Start with a waste knot and using Perle 5 #3685 in a #24 tapestry needle begin the first kloster block in the centre of the flap, refer to Chart 3a. Continue round the outer edge of the central panel. There are 47 kloster blocks down the long edge, turn stitching 90 degrees and work 11 kloster blocks, turn stitching again and work back to starting point. Now work the remaining kloster blocks on the flap.

Next work the kloster blocks across the far end of the design following chart 3b. Note they are stitched four kloster blocks from the end. Make sure the first kloster block, which is to be worked vertically, is stitched in the same holes as the horizontal kloster blocks. This will guarantee that the kloster blocks are opposite each other, see fig 1 page 61.

Handy Hint

Work the satin stitch motif on the back first, so that the one on the front flap is stitched when you are more experienced!

Following chart 3a work the kloster blocks between the two satin stitch motifs and beyond the second satin stitch design. Work the outer kloster blocks first, then the inner ones. Do this for each of the four areas.

The last kloster blocks to be worked are those round the outside of the Case. Start to the right of the kloster blocks worked on the flap and complete stitching carefully following the chart.

Double Cable

Take one thread of Wildflowers 'Royal Jewels' in a #26 tapestry needle and start by using a waste knot. Work double cable stitch (page 19) around the second satin stitch motif. Note it is only worked in the one place, round the motif on the back of the Case.

Eyelets

Using one thread of Wildflowers 'Royal Jewels' in a #26 tapestry needle work all the square and diamond eyelets (page 17). Start and finish all threads in the satin stitch and kloster blocks near the eyelets.

Buttonhole Edge Stitch

Now buttonhole stitch over four threads around the edge of the design. In this instance work between every fabric thread at all the corners. Stitch using Wildflowers 'Royal Jewels' in a #26 tapestry needle.

Cut Areas

I prefer to cut and work one section at a time. Cut the threads in the first area between the satin stitch motifs. Refer to page 20 for more information on cutting threads.

Needle Weaving

The needle weaving is worked using one thread of Wildflowers 'Royal Jewels' in a #26 needle. Start with a waste knot and begin stitching by coming up to the right of a bar and then weave over and under two threads in a figure of eight motion see page 22. To correctly work needle weaving, remember the 'step' movement (follow the arrows on the chart). Finish the thread at the back by taking working thread through completed needle weaving.

The stitching on the Case is now completed. I would recommend you stitch all items before following the finishing instructions given on page 64.

Fig 1

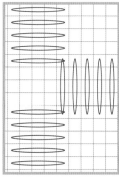

Note first stitch being worked vertically in same holes as horizontal kloster blocks

61

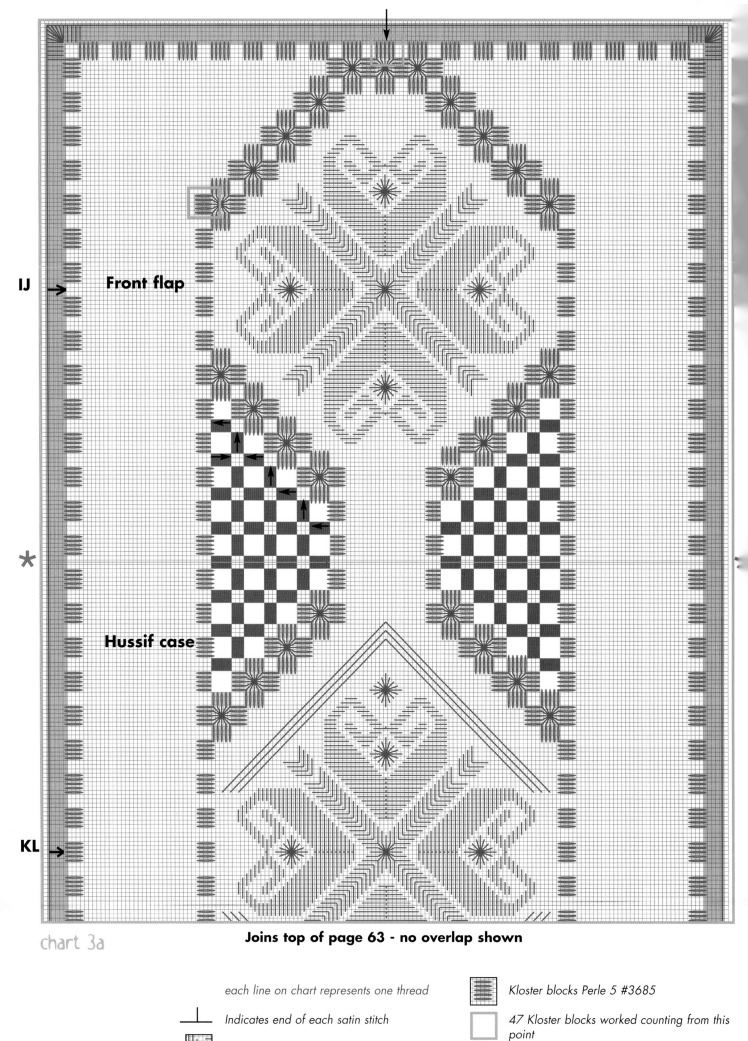

IJ → **Front flap**

✳

Hussif case

KL →

chart 3a

Joins top of page 63 - no overlap shown

each line on chart represents one thread

⊥ *Indicates end of each satin stitch*

Satin stitch Perle 5 #3685

First Kloster block worked here

Kloster blocks Perle 5 #3685

47 Kloster blocks worked counting from this point

Double Cable Wildflowers 'Royal Jewels'
KEY continued pg 63

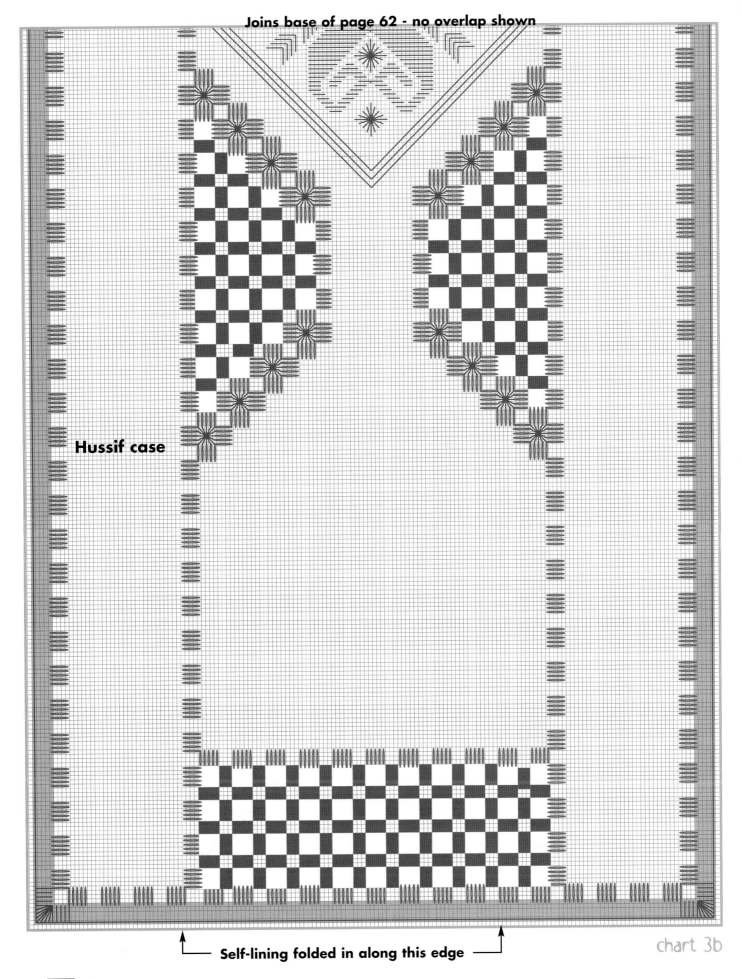

Hussif case

chart 3b

 Square eyelets Wildflowers 'Royal Jewels' → Direction of needle weaving

 Diamond eyelets Wildflowers 'Royal Jewels'   Needle weaving Wildflowers 'Royal Jewels'

Buttonhole edge stitch over four threads ∗——∗ Fold line for front flap, attach lining here
Wildflowers 'Royal Jewels'

Hussif Case

- Cut the Case out leaving a 2.5cm (1") seam allowance on all four sides including the lining *which must not be cut off,* and extends 28cm (11") beyond the buttonhole edge stitch. Neaten all newly cut edges.

- With right sides together fold the self lining in along the buttonhole edge stitch (see chart 3b). Stitch the lining to the case on each side, beginning stitching at the bottom of the embroidered section two fabric threads out from the buttonhole edge stitch. Use a matching sewing thread and a #26 tapestry needle and stitch with running or tacking stitch over two threads once at the top go back and fill in the spaces left on the way up. It is preferable to use one length of thread for both journeys. Take care not to catch the flap in the stitching and stitch only up to the position marked on chart 3a *-*. Turn the hussif right side out and slip stitch the lining neatly in place across the back of the hussif at this point.

- To form bag, fold end up to fold line for 'front flap' and with matching sewing thread and a sharp needle slip stitch the sides of the bag together.

- Now finish the flap - Cut and withdraw the thread next to the buttonhole edge stitch on all three sides. On the wrong side cut away surplus fabric along the line made by the withdrawn threads.

- Press the bag carefully using a damp cloth. Add a fastener if you wish before adding your accessories and taking it off to show your friends.

---

each line on chart represents one thread

⊥   *Indicates end of each satin stitch*

  Satin stitch Perle 5 #3685

  First Kloster blockworked here

  Kloster blocks Perle 8 #3685

   Square eyelets Wildflowers 'Royal Jewels'

   Diamond eyelets Wildflowers 'Royal Jewels'

   Buttonhole edge stitch over four threads Wildflowers 'Royal Jewels'

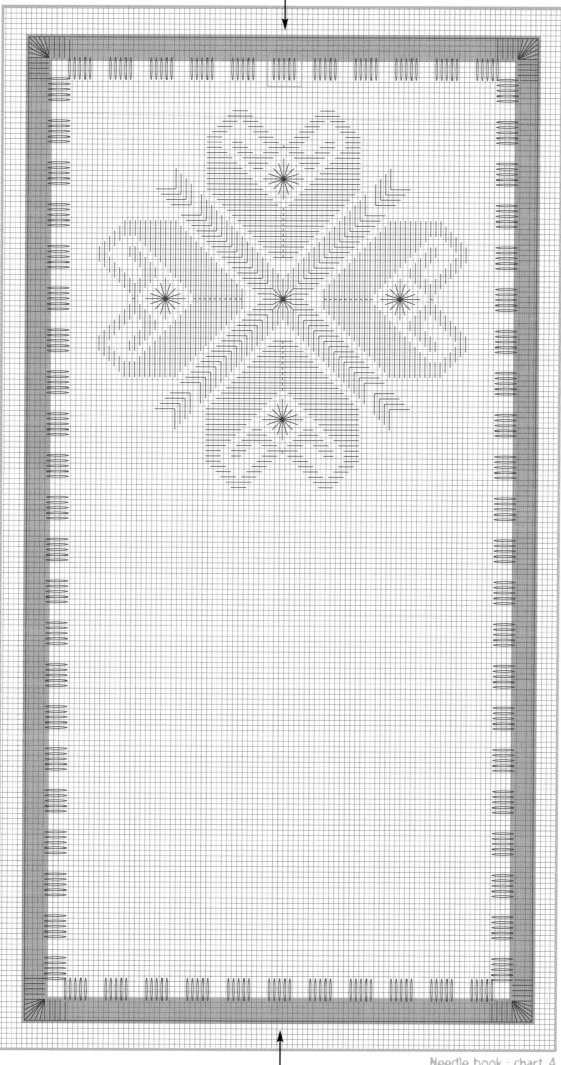

Needle book · chart 4

The Needle Book

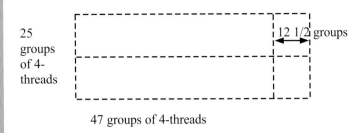

25 groups of 4-threads

12 1/2 groups

47 groups of 4-threads

With tacking thread in a #26 tapestry needle mark out the Needle Book in the area below the Case indicated in the layout diagram. It is 47 'groups' of 4-threads by 25 'groups' of 4-threads. Tack a line down the centre horizontally then count in 12½ 'groups' of 4-threads from the right hand edge and run a tacking line from the centre to each side in the usual way. This line is a guide for the placement of the satin stitch motif.

To Start

Satin Stitch Motifs

Start stitching by working the satin stitch motif on the front of the Needle Book. The tacking lines indicate its placement. Begin with a waste knot and stitch using Perle 5 #3685 in a #24 tapestry needle following chart 4.

Kloster Blocks

Next start stitching the kloster blocks. Remember each kloster block is composed of five satin stitches over four threads, refer to page 12 before you begin stitching to ensure you follow the correct stitch movement when changing direction.

Start with a waste knot and stitch following the chart using Perle 8 #3685 in a #26 tapestry needle. There are 22 kloster blocks along the long edge and 11 kloster blocks along the short edge.

Eyelets

Using one thread of Wildflowers 'Royal Jewels' in a #26 tapestry needle work all the square and diamond Eyelets. Start and finish all threads in the satin stitch near the eyelets.

Buttonhole Edge Stitch

Lastly buttonhole stitch around the edge of the design. In this instance at the corners I worked between every fabric thread on all corners. Stitch using Wildflowers in a #26 tapestry needle
Start with the back stitch method page 11.

Needle Book Making up

* Remove the thread next to the buttonhole edge stitch on all four sides.

* Turn the Needle Book to the wrong side and cut out along the line of the withdrawn thread.

* Neaten edges of two pieces of flannel 7 x 15½ cms in your preferred method (I used nun's stitch).

* Fold the Needle Book in half and place flannel pages in the centre. Using matching sewing thread in a sharp needle back stitch the pages in place working from the outside of the Needle Book and being careful to follow the grain line of the woven fabric as you stitch.

* I tied fine cord around the centre of the Needle Book and attached a small tassel as a final finishing touch!

The Scissors Holder

The scissors holder is made with two pieces of fabric, each one folded in half to form the outside and its own lining. These two pieces are then sewn together with cord stitched over the seam as a finishing touch.

Seam allowance not included.

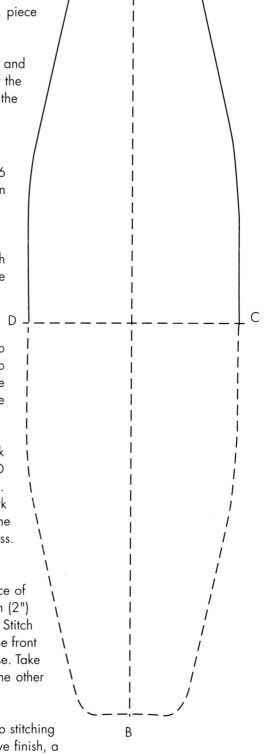

On a piece of paper, trace the scissors holder pattern. Transfer this pattern shape to the wrong side of the fabric by tracing round the pattern with a sharp pencil. With small neat stitches, tack the outline following your pencil mark then turn the work to the right side. (Allow space for a 1.5cm (½") seam allowance for each piece when placing the pattern.)

On each piece of fabric tack the centre vertically A-B over and under 4-threads in the usual way. Tack across the centre of the pattern to form a fold line C-D. Embroider on one half of the fabric only, the rest is folded down to form the lining.

To Stitch

Take one piece of fabric and using Perle 8 and a #26 tapestry needle, work the kloster blocks in the position shown on chart 5.
Change to Perle 5 and work the satin stitch motif.
Work the square and diamond eyelets using Wildflowers.
Finally still using Wildflowers work buttonhole edge stitch across the top of the kloster blocks. Repeat for the back of the scissors case on your second piece of prepared fabric.

To Construct

• The back and front are made in the same way. Cut two pieces of iron-on interfacing using the paper pattern, no seam allowance is required. Iron the interfacing to the wrong side of the lining area of the back and front of the scissors holder.

• Add a 1.5cm (½") seam allowance and cut out the back and front. With right sides together fold along line C-D and stitch along seam line with matching sewing thread. Remember to leave a section open for turning the work through. Turn the front right side out and slip stitch the opening together. Remove all tacking thread and press. Repeat for the back.

• Before stitching the back and front together, insert a piece of fine leather kid at the base of the holder. I cut mine 5 cm (2") in length and slightly narrower than the scissors holder. Stitch the first half of the leather carefully to the wrong side of the front of the scissors case at the narrow or bottom end of the case. Take care to ensure that the leather is not pulling, then sew the other half to the wrong side of the back of the scissors case.

• With right sides facing out, join the scissors holder by slip stitching down each side and across the base. To give an attractive finish, a matching cord covering the slip stitches on the three sides of the scissors case could be added.

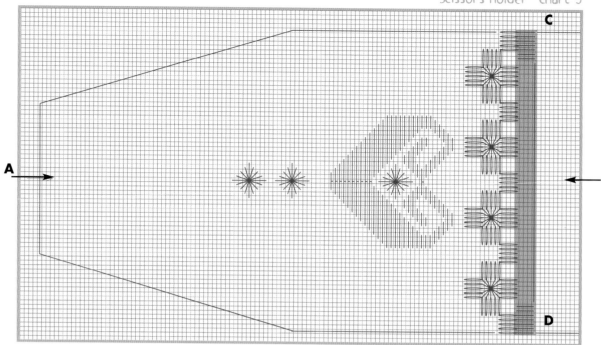

each line on chart represents one thread

⊥ Indicates end of each satin stitch

Kloster blocks Perle 8 #3685

Satin stitch Perle 5 #3685

 Square eyelets Wildflowers 'Royal Jewels'

 Diamond eyelets Wildflowers 'Royal Jewels'

Buttonhole edge stitch over four threads
Wildflowers 'Royal Jewels'

Pin Holder

The Pin Holder is made with two pieces of embroidered fabric each of which is laced over firm card. The two pieces are then stitched together with a thin piece of wool batting in between.

Cut out two circles 8cm (3¼") in diameter from firm card. Place these on the fabric and mark out and tack the fabric in the same way as for the scissors holder. Add a 2cm (¾") seam allowance round the edge of each circle.
Mark the centre of the circles vertically and horizontally by tacking over and under 4-threads in the usual way. Remember to turn your work over before you begin the embroidery.

To Start

Work the satin stitch motif in the centre of each side of the Pin Holder with Perle 5 and a #26 tapestry needle. With Wildflowers and a #26 tapestry needle work the eyelets.

To Construct

* Use the two 8cm diameter circles previously cut from firm card and on one side of each circle glue on batting. When the glue is set, cut away the surplus batting.

* Cut out your embroidered circles. REMEMBER to add a seam allowance of 2cm (¾") and run a gathering thread around the outer edge of each fabric circle.

pin holder

- Place both embroidered circles wrong sides together with the wool batting in between. With the thread of your choice, work two straight stitches through both circles twice at the same point, work a buttonhole stitch loop over these two threads. Slip along through the inside of one circle to the next point where you will repeat the process. A pearl headed pin will be slipped into the space between each group of stitches so space your stitches carefully approximately 0.5cm (¹/₄") apart.

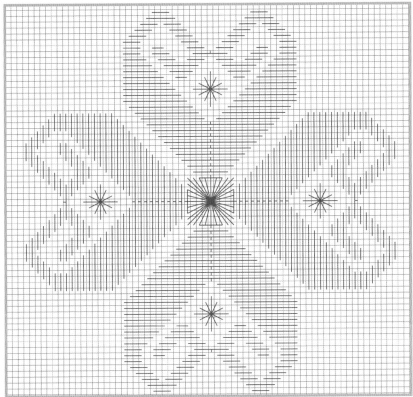

Pin holder · chart 6

each line on chart represents one thread

⊥ *Indicates end of each satin stitch*

 Satin stitch Perle 5 #3685

 Square eyelets Wildflowers 'Royal Jewels'

Diamond eyelets Wildflowers 'Royal Jewels'

Done!
Enjoy your completed project.

A Special Thought

To make sure you enjoy working these designs there are two 'musts'. First you must count accurately - hence the need for the tacking, secondly you must place your stitching and motifs accurately in each section of the design.
If you follow this advice you will avoid the need for frustrating unpicking and the consequent waste of expensive thread...

Jewellery Roll

Jewellery Roll

Here we have a project that is not only very enjoyable to stitch but also very useful for keeping those special jewellery treasures free from knocks and scratches both at home and when travelling.

To achieve a soft effect, the whole project could be worked in self colour or, as is shown, a portion could be worked in a bold contrasting colour. Personalise it to suit your taste.

Stitches Used Kloster Blocks, Satin Stitch, Square Eyelets, Double Cable Stitch, Split Wrapped Bars, Needle weaving with Picots, Oblique Loop Filling, Greek Cross Filling, Dove's Eye Filling, Buttonhole Edging Stitch variation.

Design size width 660 threads x height 210 threads, self lining a further 210 threads

Requirements

Evenweave Fabric Permin Apple Blossom 28 threads per inch, fat quarter 70 x 50cm (28 x 20")

Threads   2 x Perle 5 DMC 224 soft pink
1 x Perle 8 DMC 224 soft pink
1 x Perle 12 DMC 224 soft pink
1 skein Caron Watercolours 164 (cinnabar) use one thread at all times
1 skein Wildflowers 164 (cinnabar)
tacking thread to contrast with the background fabric
sewing thread to match the background fabric

Needles tapestry #26 and #24, sharp, crewel needle size 7

Hoop small about 12 to 15cm (5 to 6 inch)

Scissors fine, pointed and very sharp

Sundry 2 lightweight zips required, each 15cm (6"), to match background fabric

4 buttons or beads to be used as fasteners two small for the inner pockets and two larger for the outside of the Roll

To Prepare Fabric

This jewellery roll is made with one large piece of fabric folded in half lengthways so that one half is the outside of the roll and the other becomes the inside. The two ends are folded to the inside to form pockets.

Cut the fabric to 40 x 70cm. Machine neaten or hand stitch the outer edge of the fabric to prevent fraying (see Before you Begin page 9).

Layout · Jewellery Roll

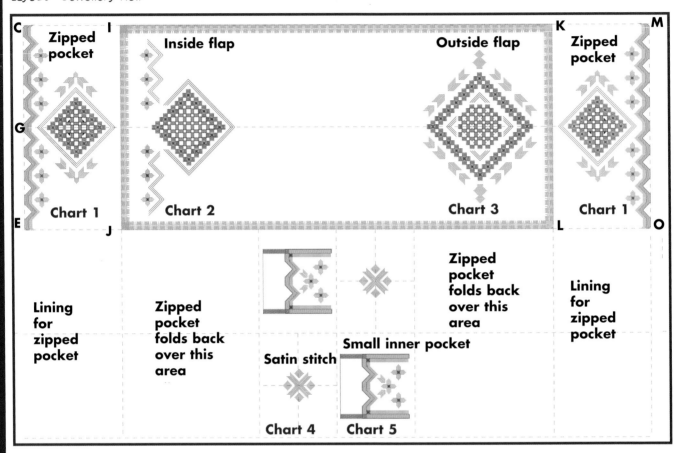

All tacking or basting is under and over four threads.

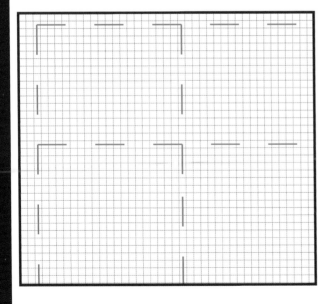

The four threads are referred to as a 'group' this makes counting much easier as you count 'groups' not individual threads. In this design the vertical tacking needs to start in the same hole as one end of the horizontal tacking, as shown. As you tack check from time to time that the stitches line up with each other. As this design is 'constructed' extra tacking is required. Accurate tacking makes it much easier to confirm accurate stitching. Hardanger, unlike some other forms of needlework, must be exact. Use a tapestry needle #26 and the contrasting tacking thread for this preparation.

Note: The instructions given here are for the fabric specified, if fabric with a different thread count is used metric and imperial measurements will need to be adjusted.

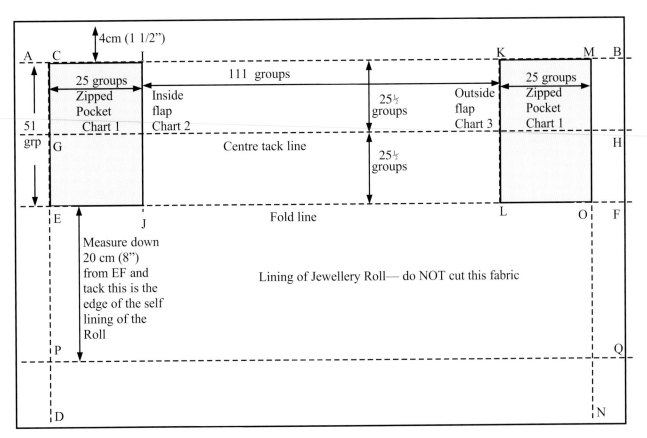

The Jewellery Roll · tacking diagram

Line AB Along one side of the 70 cm (28") edge, measure down 4 cm (1½"). With tacking thread in a #26 tapestry needle, run a tack-line over and under four threads across the fabric from edge to edge.

Line CD Count 10 'groups' along line AB, and run tack line CD down the 50 cm width of the fabric. Begin this line at the start or finish of a 4-thread group on Line AB. This line gives the left hand edge of the Jewellery Roll.

Line EF From tack line AB, count 51 'groups' down line CD and run tack line EF parallel to line AB. Make sure each 4-thread group lines up exactly to the corresponding group on line AB. This gives you the fold line for the Jewellery Roll.

Line GH From tack line AB, count 25½ 'groups' down line CD and run tack line GH. The four designs are centred along this line.

Line IJ From tack line CD count to the right along line AB 25 'groups'. Run tack line I J parallel to CD but only down to line EF. I J is one of the lines which defines the outside edge of the Jewellery Roll. A variation of Buttonhole edge stitch is from I to J, J to L, L to K and K to I.

Line KL From tack line I J count 111 'groups' and run tack line KL down to EF. The second line which defines the outside edge of the Jewellery Roll.

Line MN From tack line KL, count 25 groups and run tack line MN the full width of the fabric.

Line PQ From the line EF measure down 20cm (8") and run a tack line across the width of the fabric. The area beyond EF is the self lining for the jewellery roll. Do NOT cut this fabric off. With the tacking completed you are now on to the 'fun' part! The embroidery is so much easier with this tacking framework established.

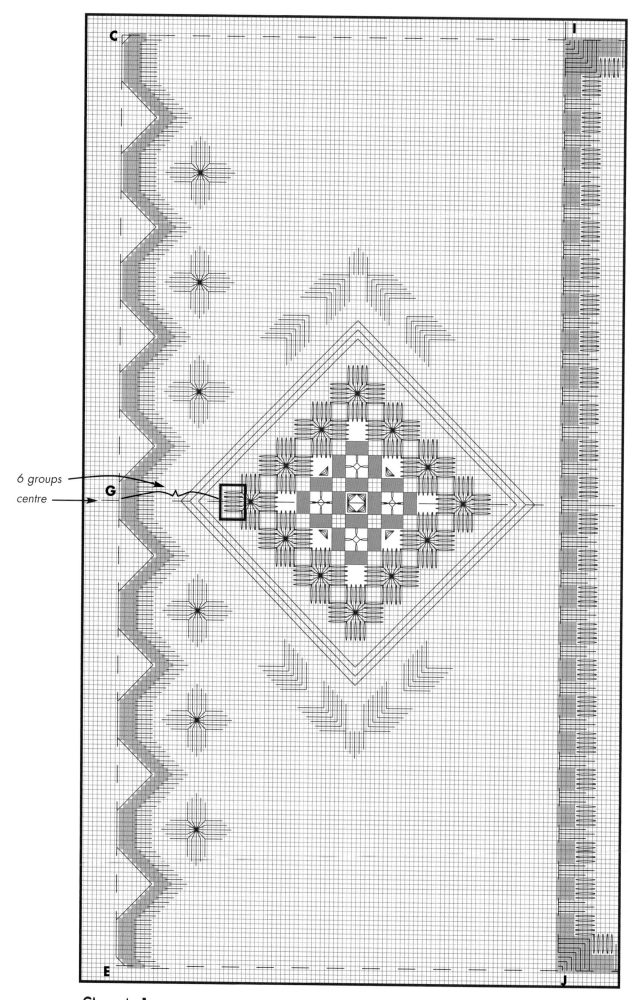

6 groups

centre

Chart 1   Zipped Internal Pockets design

- worked at each end of the fabric design at base of photo page 70.

Zipped Internal Pockets · Chart 1

The zipped embroidered pockets are worked at each end - the shaded areas CIJE and KMOL - see tacking diagram page 73.

Kloster Blocks

These are stitched using a #24 tapestry needle and Watercolours 'cinnabar'. Start with a waste knot and centre the first kloster block over the horizontal tacked line as shown in the chart, continue from this point. For more information on stitching kloster blocks refer to page 12.

Double Cable & Eyelets

Diagonal cable stitch (page 19) and the square eyelets inside the kloster blocks are worked using Caron Wildflowers 'cinnabar' in a #26 tapestry needle.

Satin Stitch

With a #24 tapestry needle and Watercolours 'cinnabar', work the satin stitch pattern at the top and bottom of the diamond. Start with a waste knot.

The pocket edge is outlined with a row of satin stitch worked over four threads in a 'wave' pattern see chart. Stitch this and the flowers along the edge using Perle 5 #224 'soft pink' and a #24 tapestry needle in the area indicated on the graph.

Eyelets

For the square eyelets at the centre of the flowers, use Perle 12 #224 'soft pink' and a #26 tapestry needle. To start and finish your thread, work it through the back of each flower. Do not carry threads across the work or over eyelet openings.

Buttonhole Edge Stitch

Work buttonhole edge stitch over four threads beyond the 'wavey' satin stitch, repeating the 'wave' design, using Perle 8 and 224 'soft pink' and a #26 tapestry needle.

Filling Stitches

To work the filling stitches, begin by cutting the necessary fabric threads, refer to page 20 for more information on cutting threads. Use very fine sharp pointed scissors. With Wildflowers #264 'cinnabar' and a #26 tapestry needle, work the filling stitches. At this point I chose to work Greek Cross page 26 and Dove's Eye filling page 25 over split wrapped bars. Do choose the filling stitches you enjoy stitching when making your jewellery roll.

each line on chart represents one thread

Although tacking is shown here, in reality it is removed before doing needleweaving

☐ *Start working first Kloster block here*

Kloster blocks - Watercolours 'cinnabar'

Double cable - Wildflowers 'cinnabar'

Square eyelets inside Kloster blocks - Wildflowers 'cinnabar'

 Satin stitch top and bottom of diamond Watercolours 'cinnabar', Satin stitch 'flowers' and pocket edge Perle 5 soft pink

 Square eyelet at centre of satin stitch flowers Perle 12 soft pink

 Buttonhole edge stitch Perle 8 soft pink

 Split wrapped bars - Wildflowers 'cinnabar'

Greek cross - Wildflowers 'cinnabar' Where a quarter of the Pattern is Shown -It is only Worked in that Corner

 Dove's eye - Wildflowers 'cinnabar'

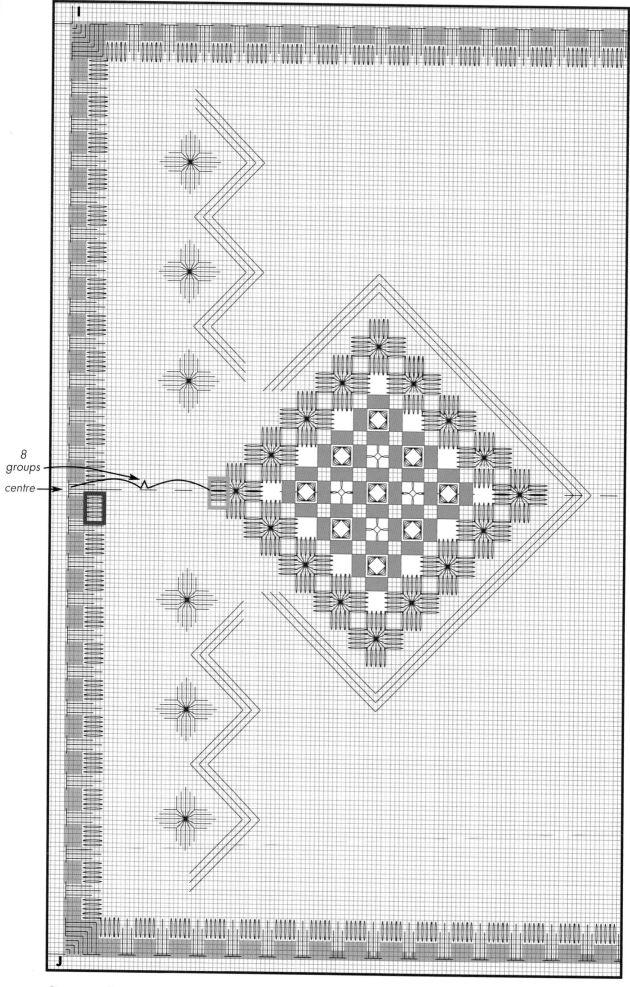

8
groups

centre

Chart 2   Self coloured Design - inside flap

- worked next to the zipped pocket design at one end, refer to the layout diagram page 72, not shown on photograph.

Self Coloured Design - inside flap - Chart 2

This stitched area is worked to the right of tack line IJ.

Kloster Blocks

Following the chart work the outer row of kloster blocks first using Perle 5 #224 'soft pink' and a #24 tapestry needle. Start with a waste knot. Complete by working the inner row of kloster blocks. Still using the same needle and thread complete the six satin stitch flowers.

Eyelets & Double Cable Stitch

The square eyelets (page 17) and double cable stitch (page 19) are worked using Perle 12 #224 'soft pink' and a #26 tapestry needle. Start with a waste knot and finish by weaving through the back of the stitched areas.

Filling Stitch

Prepare work for filling stitches, (refer to page 20 for Cutting Threads). Using Perle 8 #224 'soft pink' and a #26 tapestry needle, work the filling stitches. At this point I chose to work Greek Cross (page 26) and Dove's eyes (page 25) over split wrapped bars.

Split Wrapped Bars

Split wrapped bars are worked by dividing four threads into two pairs. Within the square to be filled, wrap each bar until you are midway along the last bar. Work the Dove's eye in the usual way. Then finish by wrapping to the end of the last bar.

each line on chart represents one thread

Although tacking is shown here, in reality it is removed before doing needleweaving

Start working first Kloster block here

Kloster blocks - Perle 5 soft pink

Satin stitch - Perle 5 soft pink

Square eyelets and centre of flowers - Perle 12 soft pink

Double cable - Perle 12 soft pink

 Split wrapped bars - Perle 8 soft pink

 Greek cross - Perle 8 soft pink

 Dove's eye - Perle 8 soft pink

 Start Kloster block edging here

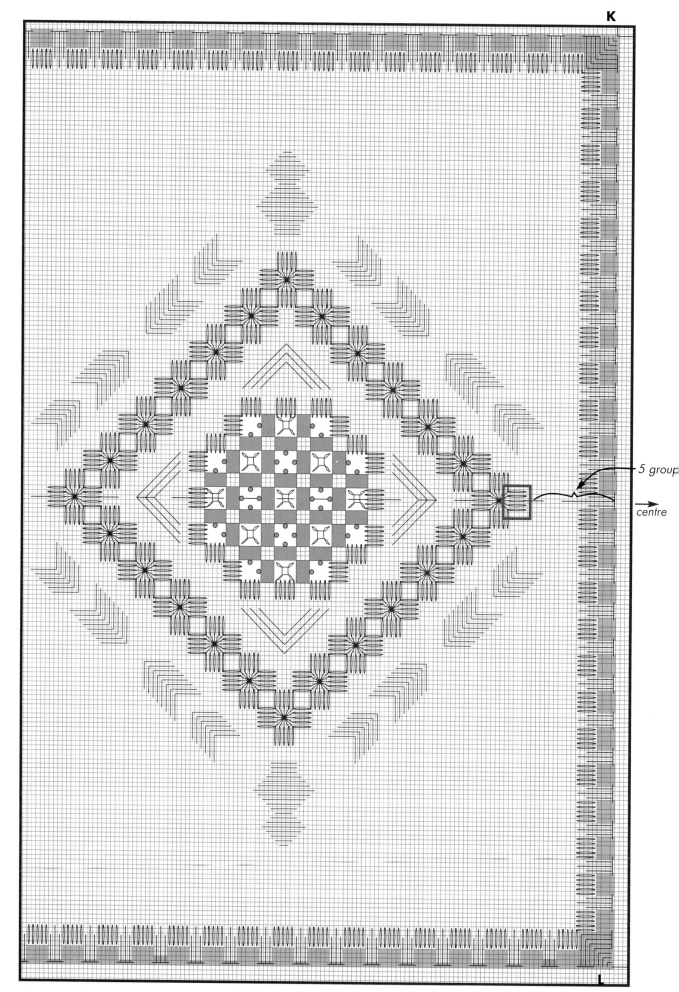

K

5 group

centre

L

Chart 3 Large wine coloured design- Outside flap

- at top of photo page 70 be worked adjacent to the zipped pocket design at the opposite end to Chart 2. This is the outer embroidered area of the jewellery roll.

Large wine coloured design · Outside flap · Chart 3

This stitched area is worked to the left of tack line KL.

Kloster Blocks & Satin Stitch

Following the chart work the outer row of kloster blocks (page 12) using Watercolours 'cinnabar' and a #24 tapestry needle. Start with a waste knot. Complete both the outer and inner rows of kloster blocks forming the outer diamond plus the kloster blocks for the inner pattern. With the same needle and thread, work the satin stitch motif pattern around the edge of the kloster block diamond.

Double Cable & Eyelets

The short rows of double cable stitch (page 19), worked at the four points of the inner pattern, are worked with Wildflowers 'cinnibar' and a #26 tapestry needle as are the square eyelets (page 17).

Filling Stitches

Cut threads in preparation for filling stitches (page 20). Using Wildflowers 'cinnibar' and a #26 tapestry needle, work the filling stitches. At this point I chose to work needle weaving incorporating oblique loop filling and picots, refer to the chart for their placement. Do choose the fillings you prefer.

The Edging

With all four embroidered areas stitched, now work the kloster blocks and buttonhole edge stitch variation that marks the outer edge of the jewellery roll.

This is worked within the area I J L K . Refer back to Chart 2 page 76. Start at the horizontal centre tack line by stitching two fabric threads to the right of the centre tack line and four fabric threads in from line I J . (The first kloster block to be worked is marked on the chart). To work the kloster blocks, use Perle 5 #224 'soft pink' and a #24 tapestry needle.
There are 24 kloster blocks across the roll and 54 kloster blocks down each side. Complete by working buttonhole edge stitch variation using Perle 12 #224 'soft pink' and a #26 tapestry needle. Note the long stitches that are taken between each of the kloster blocks and follow the graph carefully when turning the corners. Once completed, this makes an attractive and interesting edge to the jewellery roll.

Buttonhole edge stitch variation with corner

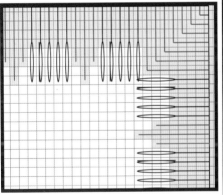

each line on chart represents one thread

Start here for Kloster block diamond

Kloster blocks - Watercolours 'cinnabar'

Satin stitch - Watercolours 'cinnabar'

Cable stitch - Wildflowers 'cinnabar'

Square eyelets - Wildflowers 'cinnabar'

Needle weaving - Wildflowers 'cinnabar'

Picots - Wildflowers 'cinnabar'

Oblique loops - Wildflowers 'cinnabar'

Kloster blocks around outer edge - Perle 5 soft pink

Buttonhole edge stitch variation - Perle 12 soft pink

Chart 4

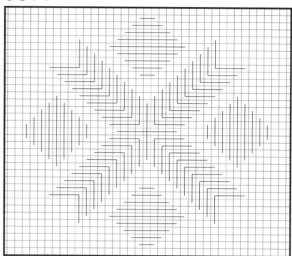

Satin stitch motifs · Chart 4

Before assembling your jewellery roll, you may like to include the additional embroidered motif given or perhaps additional pockets. Work the satin stitch motif in Perle 5 soft pink and a #24 needle. See Construction notes for the best time to stitch this. They can be used beside the small pockets inside the Jewellery Roll see photo page 70.

Small Inner Pockets · Chart 5

Mark out two inner pockets 20 x 10cm (8 x 4inch) on the unused fabric beneath the jewellery roll lining. Find the centre lengthways and work a tack line over and under four threads using contrasting tacking thread and #26 tapestry needle for 45 'groups' of 4-threads.

Chart 5

Small Inner Pockets

- inside Jewellery Roll see photo page 70

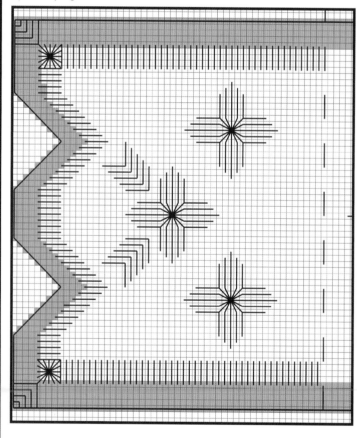

Mark a point 2.5cm (1") in from the edge of the fabric. Count 12 'groups' from this point and run a tack line across the 10cm (4in) width. From this tack line, count a further 17 'groups' and run another tack line then a final one 16 'groups' away from the last tack line.

The embroidery for each pocket is worked in the 12 'group' section following Chart 5.

Satin Stitch

Begin by working the flowers and leaves in satin stitch using Perle 5 #224 'soft pink' and a #24 tapestry needle.

Eyelets

Change to Perle 12 #224 'soft pink' and a #26 tapestry needle and work the square eyelets (page 17).

Satin Stitch Border

Next work the satin stitch border for each pocket flap using Perle 5 #224 'soft pink and a #24 tapestry needle.

Note - the satin stitch is worked only in this 12-thread group area and is worked over four fabric threads inside the buttonhole edge stitch.

Buttonhole Edge Stitch

Work buttonhole edge stitch over four threads using Perle 12 #224 'soft pink' and a #26 tapestry needle right round the entire pocket (that is 45 'groups' in length and 16 'groups' in width). Complete the embroidery by working a square eyelet in the corners between the satin stitch and the buttonhole edge stitch, still using the Perle 12.

each line on chart represents one thread

Satin stitch flowers - Perle 5 soft pink

Square eyelets - Perle 12 soft pink

Satin stitch border - Perle 5 soft pink

Buttonhole edge - Perle 12 soft pink

Construction

Small Inner Pockets

• To cut small pockets from the main piece of fabric - begin by withdrawing the fabric thread adjacent to the worked buttonhole stitch on both pockets.

• From the wrong side cut along this withdrawn thread. Use very sharp, fine pointed scissors for this and take care to cut each thread individually. You do not wish to slip and cut your embroidery! Take your time, don't hurry, concentrate. If you are doing this type of cutting for the first time, try and do it when you are fresh. With the pulled out thread to guide you, you will find it really is quite straightforward. Refer to page 55 for cutting the uneven edge.

• To close each pocket, fold along the fold line. Before stitching the small pockets on to the jewellery roll, add a button or bead and a hand made looped buttonhole for closing. At this stage the sides of the pocket are still open - they are closed when they are attached to the Jewellery Roll.

Tacking Diagram

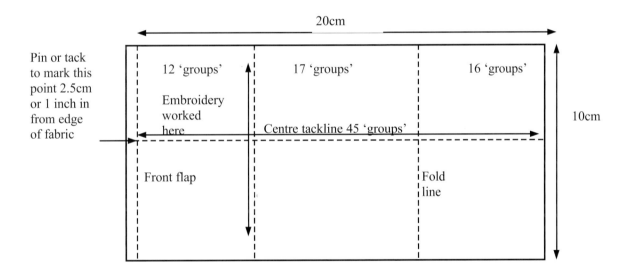

Completion of Jewellery Roll

- On all four sides, this includes the lining of the jewellery roll, mark a 4cm (1$^{1}/_{2}$ ") seam allowance. The section where the lining joins the embroidered roll will be a folded edge - *this must not be cut off at any time.* Trim the four edges and then neaten.

- Placement of the small inner pockets and the optional satin stitch motif was sorted out by 'eye'. Fold the fabric along the buttonhole edge stitch to establish the finished size of the Jewellery Roll and with this as a guide stitch the satin stitch motifs and place the two pockets in the central area of the lining, if desired. One pocket is seen in the photo page 70 and the other is above it diagonally to the left. Attach the pockets to the lining with back stitch over two threads just inside the buttonhole edge stitch. Use a 'sharp' needle and matching sewing thread and take care not to catch down the pocket flaps.

- In the middle area behind the small inner pockets I added a very fine piece of batting (13.5 x 15cm 5$^{1}/_{4}$ x 6") Centre the batting in this area then carefully tack into place. Remember to exclude the seam allowance when cutting the batting. This was attached to the jewellery roll using a 'sharp' needle and matching sewing thread. These stitches should not show on the right side of your work.

- With the right sides facing, fold the jewellery roll in half along line EF (the 'fold line'). With your 'sharp' #7 needle, matching thread and following a thread of the woven fabric, stitch the long side of the roll together. Work two fabric threads outside the buttonhole edge stitch. *Do not stitch the ends closed at this stage.*

- Turn through.

- Turn up each end pocket along the buttonhole edge stitch. Lightly press along this edge. Measure 9cm (3$^{1}/_{2}$ ") from the folded edge and mark the centre of the lining, also mark the centre of the zip. Match these centres, pin one half of open zip to the lining taking care to have the fabric edge of the zip facing down to the folded edge of the pocket.

- By slipping your hand up through the open end, stitch this half of the zip into place.

- Four fabric threads out from the 'wavey' buttonhole edge stitch on the pocket, turn in the seam allowance.

- Match the centre of the pocket with the centre of the second half of the zip. With your 'sharp' #7 needle and matching sewing thread, stitch the zip into place with back stitch over two threads. Stitch two fabric threads away from the embroidery.

- Fold surplus lining fabric in and slip stitch into place on the inside of the zip.

- Slip stitch the sides of the zipped pockets together and any small opening visible at the top.

- To help with opening and closing the zips you may like to add a small tassel.

- Remove any tacking that may still be in place.

- Fold your roll and to help it stay closed, add beads or buttons and loops of your choice.

Your jewellery will now travel safely and securely in this delightful Roll made especially for the purpose.

Work bag & accessories

Work Bag & Accessories

This design is for you! Enjoy working and making this special Work Bag that is so practical yet so attractive. The natural linen background is a foil for the attractive variegated threads which create a bright and lively appearance. Working through this project will be exciting as you personalise it to your special requirements.

Stitches used Kloster Blocks, Buttonhole Edge Stitch, Eyelets, Diagonal and Straight Cable Stitch, Needle Weaving with Dove's Eyes, Hemstitch, Buttonhole Stitch, Satin Stitch

Design size width 700 threads x height 380 threads

Requirements

Fabric Cashel 28 threads per inch, Natural Colour, two fat quarters each 70 x 50cm (20 x 28") or one piece of fabric 50 x 140 cm (20 x 56")

Lining fabric cotton to tone with the bag fabric or threads used, one metre (one and a quarter yards)

Threads 3 skeins Caron Watercolours 'Ruby' use one thread at all times
1 skein Caron Wildflowers thread 'Ruby'
1 ball Perle 8 DMC 820 royal blue
1 ball Perle 12 to match Cashel fabric (for hemstitching)
Contrasting sewing cotton for tacking
Sewing thread to match background fabric

Needles Tapestry sizes 22, 24, 26 and a Sharp

Card heavy weight, two pieces for the base of the bag 18cm (7") diameter. Medium weight two pieces for the pincushion 8cm (3") diameter

Padding lightweight dacron for inner base of bag and for both pincushion circles.

Small quantity of fibrefill or unspun wool for the scissors pincushion.

Wool flannel one or more pieces for the needle case, 18 x 10 cm (7 x 4")

Embroidery hoop 10 - 12 cm (4 - 5")

Scissors fine pointed embroidery (and very sharp!)

Pins a packet, pearl headed

Pencil HB (and sharp)

Fine cord 160cm (63 inches) bought commercially or hand made (I used 3 skeins Perle 5 DMC 820 royal blue)

Iron on interfacing 15 x 8 cm (6 x 3¼")

Craft glue

Note: *The instructions given here are for the fabric specified, if fabric with a different thread count is used metric and imperial measurements will need to be adjusted.*

General Preparation

There are four separate parts to the work bag. One fat quarter will be used for the bag and the second fat quarter is used for the base of the bag and for the accessories. A layout diagram for the placement for the base and accessories is shown on page 97.

- Work bag (made using first fat quarter)
- Needle Book
- Pin holder
- Scissor case
- Outer base of Bag

} (made using the second fat quarter)

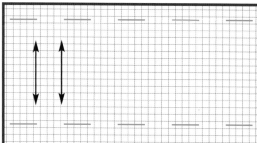

Neaten the raw edges of fabric to prevent fraying, see 'Before you Begin' page 9.

All tacking is under and over four threads.
The four threads are referred to as a 'group', this makes counting much easier as you count 'groups', not individual threads.
When working rows of tacking, make sure that each tacking stitch lines up the with the stitch in the lines above and below as shown. To check, run the blunt end of a needle down the fabric by following the thread of the woven linen from the base of a 'group' on one tack line, to the base of a 'group' on the next tack line. As this design is 'constructed' extra tacking is required. Accurate tacking makes it much easier to confirm accurate stitching. Hardanger, unlike some other forms of needlework, must be exact. Use a tapestry needle #26 and the contrasting tacking thread for this preparation.

Work Bag

Preparation

Take one fat quarter, a #26 tapestry needle and contrasting tacking thread and begin!

Work bag tacking diagram
Not to scale

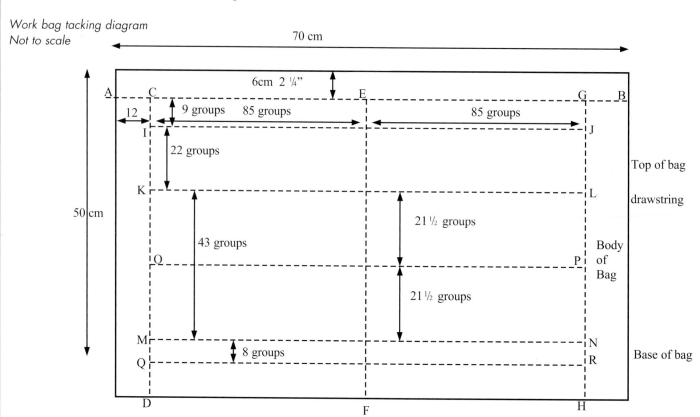

- **Line AB** Along one side of the 70cm (28") edge, measure in 6cm (2¼"). Run a tack line over and under four threads across the fabric from edge to edge. The top row of Kloster Blocks, for the edging, come up to here - buttonhole edging stitch is worked beyond this.

Begin the following tacklines CD, EF and GH at the start or finish of a 4-thread group on line AB.

- **Line CD** Count 12 'groups' to the right along line AB. Begin tack line CD at the start or finish of a 4-thread group on line AB and tack down the 50 cm width of the fabric. This line gives the left hand edge of the bag.

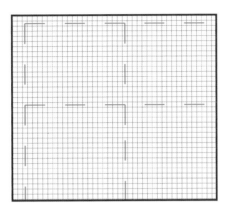

Note: Stitches start at the beginning or end of a 4-thread group

- **Line EF** From tack line CD, count 85 'groups' to the right along line AB and stitch tack line EF. This line marks the vertical centre of the design. Again start tacking at the start or finish of a 4-thread group on line AB

- **Line GH** From tack line EF, count 85 'groups' to the right along line AB and run tack line GH. This line gives the right hand edge of the bag. You will now have three vertical tack lines (CD, EF, GH) across your fabric. Make sure each 4-thread group starts and finishes at the same thread on these three tack lines.

Begin the following tack lines IJ, KL, MN and QR at the start or finish of a 4-thread group on line CD.

- **Line IJ** On line CD where tack lines CD and AB meet, count down 9 groups and run tack line I J . The top row of Kloster Blocks for the edging come down to here.

- **Line KL** From I J count down 22 groups and run tack line KL. The top row of hem stitch for the drawstring is worked along this line.

- **Line MN** From KL count down 43 groups and run tack line MN. The straight cable stitch is worked along this line and the Satin Stitch chevron design is worked below.

- **Line QR** From MN count down 8 groups and run tack line QR. The bottom of the bag is attached to the circular base below this line.

- **Line OP** Find the centre between KM and LN and run tack line OP. Centre the diamond designs on this line. This line will start in the middle of a 'group'.

The front and the back of the bag are in one piece.

Handy Hint

Write the letters for the different tack lines on to pieces of paper and sew or safety pin them to your fabric for easy reference

Work bag fig 1

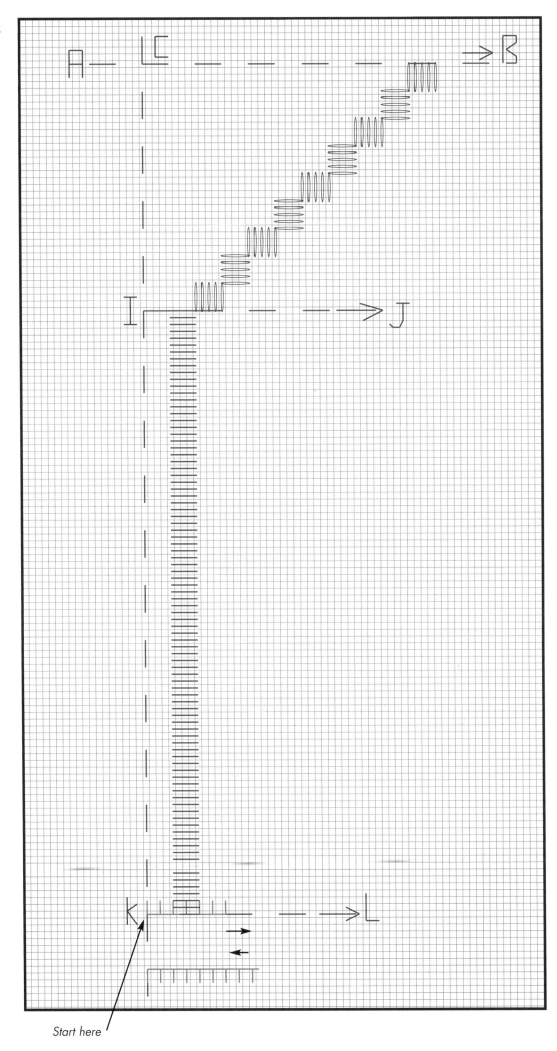

Start here

Top of bag

To Stitch:

Work the top of the bag first - the edging. To make the edging fall nicely and give easy access to the contents of the bag the 'edging' opens down to the drawstring on each side. To allow for this there is a band of buttonhole edge stitch (worked later) then a band of Satin Stitch. This is worked over four threads *on top of* the first row of hemstitching which is worked first of all. Refer to chart *work bag fig 1.*

Now to start!

Along tack line KL, using Perle 12 (to match the linen) and #26 tapestry needle begin by working the first row of hem stitching. Start at K and work over two fabric threads to L. Turn fabric around to work your second row of hemstitching which is started two 'groups' (8-threads) away from the first completed row. This second row begins 8 threads below L and finishes 8 threads below K. Make sure the threads wrapped in the second row lie opposite the threads wrapped in the first row so that it is easy to thread the drawstring cord through when the bag is completed.

Satin Stitch & Kloster blocks

Thread a #22 tapestry needle with Caron Watercolours 'ruby' and starting with a waste knot work the first row of Satin Stitch over four fabric threads. Begin stitching four threads to the right of K, (working on top of the hem stitch) changing to Kloster Blocks when line I J is reached. Refer to chart *work bag fig 1.*

each line on chart represents one thread

 Hemstitch over two threads worked from k-l Left to right, second row from right to left (invert your work). Stitch using matching Perle 12

 Satin stitch over 4-threads - Watercolours 'ruby'

 Kloster blocks - Watercolours 'ruby'

(Buttonhole edge stitch worked later between tack line and satin stitch)

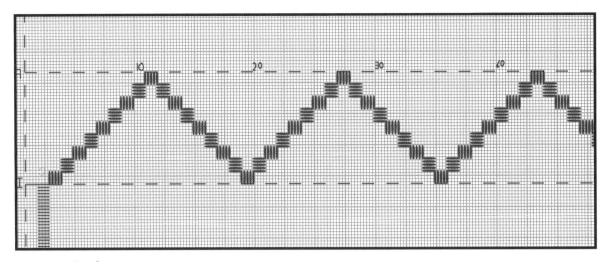

Work bag Fig 2

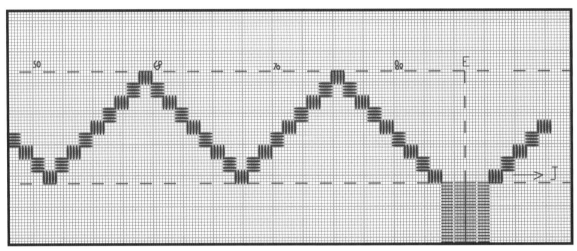

Work bag Fig 2 · continued   **There is no overlap shown on these charts**

each line on chart represents one thread

 Satin stitch over 4 threads - Watercolours 'ruby'

 Kloster blocks - Watercolours 'ruby'

 Buttonhole edge stitch over 4 threads - shown but not stitched at this point

Follow this first (outer) row of Kloster Blocks to a position two 'groups' before the centre tack line EF finishing the Kloster Blocks at the line I J . You will have formed five Kloster Block peaks and have now worked one half of the bag. Work bag fig 2.

At this point still using the same needle and thread change to Satin Stitch worked over four threads and stitch down to line KL. Finish your thread off. Leave eight threads (buttonhole edging stitch will be worked here later) then with a new thread work a further row of Satin Stitch over four threads up to I J then work the second half of the bag top in the area marked out.

Work the second and third rows of Kloster Blocks using the same needle and thread see *Work bag fig 3*.

Cable Stitch

Beneath the third row of double Kloster Blocks diagonal double cable stitch (page 19) is worked. This emphasises and defines the edging. Use a #26 tapestry needle and Perle #8 'Royal Blue'. Begin with a waste knot and finish by working into the back of the work.

Buttonhole Edge Stitch

Buttonhole Edge Stitch can now be worked outside the previously completed Satin Stitch to form the opening for the 'edging' at each side and across the top of the bag beyond the Kloster Blocks, forming a firm finished edge to this section of the bag. Buttonhole Edge Stitch (page 15) is stitched over four threads using a #26 tapestry needle and Perle #8 'Royal Blue'. To start, thread through the base of the Satin Stitch band at one side. When turning an outer corner, work a buttonhole stitch into each thread of the fabric. For an inner corner, only one stitch is made.

Eyelets

Work eyelets using a #26 tapestry needle and Perle 8 DMC 820 'Royal Blue'. Work two rows across the top edge, their placement is shown on the chart. To start and finish, work by threading through already completed Kloster Blocks.

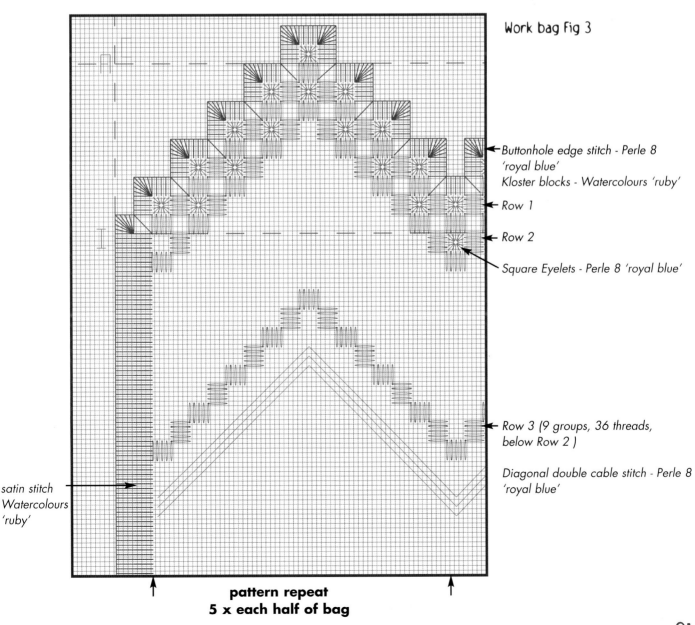

Work bag Fig 3

← Buttonhole edge stitch - Perle 8 'royal blue'
Kloster blocks - Watercolours 'ruby'

← Row 1

← Row 2

← Square Eyelets - Perle 8 'royal blue'

← Row 3 (9 groups, 36 threads, below Row 2)

Diagonal double cable stitch - Perle 8 'royal blue'

satin stitch Watercolours 'ruby'

pattern repeat
5 x each half of bag

BODY OF BAG

Diamonds
chart (diamond) see Work bag fig 4 page 93

There are four diamonds worked on the body of the bag. Centre the first Diamond on the horizontal tack line OP and vertical tack line EF Work the complete design including the diagonal double cable stitch. From the *point of the cable stitch* count $13^{1}/_{2}$ 'groups' (54 threads) to the right and to the left along line OP and work a further diamond. The fourth and final diamond is worked in two halves with one half adjacent to line CD and the other half adjacent to line GH, again centre on line OP. Work the satin stitch which straddles the seam line once the seam has been joined.

placement of full and half diamonds on body of bag (not to scale)

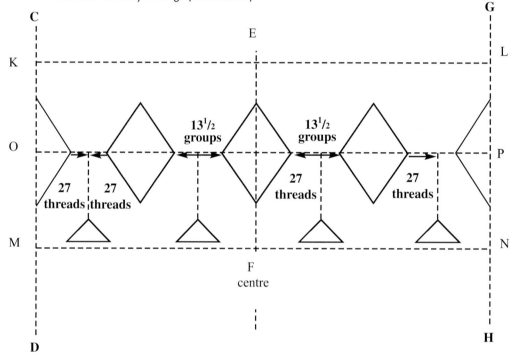

Work bag tacking diagram for reference shaded area 'body of bag'

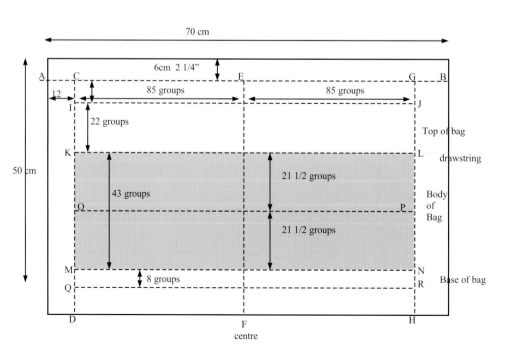

Work bag fig 4

each line on chart represents one thread

⊥ *Indicates end of each satin stitch*

Satin stitch - Watercolours 'ruby'

Kloster blocks - Watercolours 'ruby'

Square eyelets Perle 8 - royal blue

Double cable - Perle 8 royal blue

Satin stitch & Kloster blocks

Start with a waste knot and work the Satin Stitch motif at the centre of the diamond, then work the Kloster Blocks. These are all stitched using a #22 tapestry needle and Caron Watercolours 'ruby'.

Eyelets

Work the Square Eyelet in the centre of each Kloster Block with a #26 tapestry needle and Perle 8 'royal blue'. Start and finish by threading through Kloster Blocks.

Cable stitch

Following the chart for its placement, work Double Cable stitch beyond the Kloster Blocks to form the diamond outline. Use a #26 tapestry needle and Perle 8 'royal blue'.

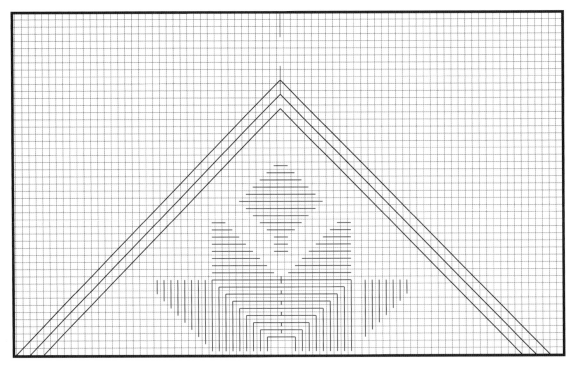

Half Diamonds

See chart work bag fig 5
for placement see Body of bag 92

Work bag Fig 5

each line on chart represents one thread

⊥ Indicates end of each satin stitch

▦ Satin stitch - Watercolours 'ruby'

▨ Double cable - Perle 8 royal blue

Centre these between the four Diamonds on the body of the bag. Count 27 threads from the point of the cable stitch and add a further tack line or run your needle down the fabric to find the starting position which is six threads above tack line MN. Use the same needles and threads as were used for the Diamonds.

Base of bag

Straight Cable stitch (page 18) is worked along tack line MN beginning at the vertical tack line CD. Complete the row at tack line GH. It is stitched using a #24 tapestry needle and Perle 8 'royal blue' beginning with a waste knot. Next work the satin stitch which forms the base of the design using a #22 tapestry needle, Caron Watercolours 'ruby' and beginning with a waste knot. Centre the design over EF 6 threads below tack line MN and above tack line QR. Repeat working to the left and right. This design will not meet at the seam line - this space is designed for your initials and date. See *work bag fig 6*.

Work bag Fig 6

Design around base of bag. Centre over tack-in EF & work to left & right

each line on chart represents one thread

⊥ *Indicates end of each satin stitch*

Cable stitch is worked along line MN - Perle 8 'royal blue' (not shown)

▦ *Satin stitch - Watercolours 'ruby'*

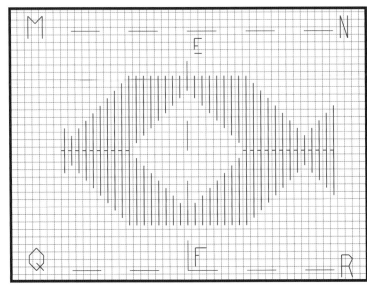

Work bag fig 7

each line on chart represents one thread

 Satin stitch over 4 threads - watercolours 'ruby'

 Kloster blocks - Watercolours 'ruby'

Buttonhole edge stitch - Perle 8 'royal blue'

Double cable stitch - Perle 8 'royal blue'

 Square eyelets - Perle 8 'royal blue'

 Needle weaving Wildflowers 'ruby'

 Dove's eye - Wildflowers 'ruby'

Tacking is left here as a guide it would of course be removed before needleweaving

Top of bag

Cutting the threads

Cut the threads in the area indicated on the chart along the top of the bag. When working a large area, only cut and withdraw enough threads to fit within your hoop. Cut the threads carefully. Refer to page 20 for more information on cutting threads.

Needle weaving with Dove's Eye Filling

Needle weaving has been combined with three rows of Dove's eye filling stitched using Caron Wildflowers 'ruby' in a #26 tapestry needle - see chart for placement of Dove's Eye Filling. Any filling stitch could be worked - choose your favourite and complete the whole area of needle weaving. For more information on needle weaving see page 22, for Dove's Eye filling see page 25.

Construction

- From the Satin Stitch pattern at the base of the bag, measure down 3 cm (1¼") and cut away the surplus fabric. From the side edges of the body of the bag, measure out 1.5 cm (½"). Cut away surplus fabric. Neaten these three raw edges with thread to match the bag.

- Next cut away surplus fabric at the side of the bag. Begin by removing the thread adjacent to the buttonhole edge stitch down each side to the point where the second row of hem stitching began and finished along lines I K and J L . With sharp fine-pointed scissors, cut off surplus fabric along the line formed by the withdrawn thread. Cut from the wrong side.

- Continue cutting across the stepped buttonhole edge stitch at the top of the Work Bag. In this instance leave one fabric thread adjacent to the buttonhole edge stitch and cut away the fabric between this fabric thread and the next. Once completed at each inner corner there will be two little threads hanging, cut them off. To match the opening of the frill down from E along line EF on the wrong side, cut each individual fabric thread down to the TOP of the hemstitching. This is best done in the daylight when you are fresh.

- There is only one seam to stitch the bag together. Using the vertical tack lines at each end of the bag as your guide, match the embroidered areas so that the embroidery appears seamless. To achieve this accuracy stitch this seam by hand with a #26 tapestry needle and matching sewing cotton. Work from the end of the second row of hem stitch to the cut bottom edge of the bag. Put this to one side whilst you prepare the base and lining.

Second fat quarter

The outer base for the bag along with the needle case, pin holder and the scissors cushion are all cut out of the second fat quarter, see layout diagram 2.

Outer Base for Bag

Cut two circles out of heavy weight card 18cm (7") in diameter. One base will be laced with the embroidery fabric, the second with the lining. I glued a piece of light weight dacron to the circle to be covered with lining so that the inside of the bag would be a little softer - this is entirely optional. Make sure the cut edge for both circles is smooth, a light rub with a piece of fine sandpaper will help.

Place a card circle on the fabric as a pattern and trace round it with a pencil. Allow an additional 5 cm (2") outside the marked circle for a seam/lacing allowance and cut here. The cut fabric circle is about 28cm diameter overall. Turn the circle over so that the marked pencil line is on the wrong side. Run a gathering thread around the outer edge of the seam allowance. Pull the gathering thread up with one cardboard circle inside. Lace firmly around the circle keeping the cardboard neatly centred on the pencil line. Put to one side.

Second fat quarter - layout diagram 2

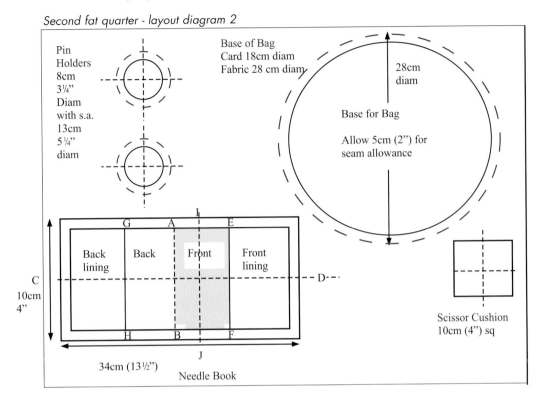

The Lining

To cut the lining for your bag, measure the width of your bag including seam allowances. Mine was 61cm (24") and the depth needs to be 44 cm (17 ¾"). This allows for the folding and forming of the pockets. With the right side of the fabric facing you, measure from the bottom edge 24cm (9½") and mark this line with a pin along the length of the fabric. Fold the fabric on this pin line. As you press this fold line remove the pins. Now fold the raw edge of the fabric down to lie on the just pressed fold line forming a three layered hem which is 12 cm (4¾") deep. Press this new fold line. These pockets are very deep as the bottom of the pocket is gathered with the bag and stitched to the base.

Across the lining through this hem make pockets to hold your embroidery requirements. To do this, stitch top to bottom through the hem making different sized pockets. Remember to allow a little extra width for ease.

- Attach the lining to the embroidered bag just below the lower row of hem stitch. Take care to get right and wrong sides sorted out!
- Sew the side seams of the lining together.
- Turn the lining down inside the bag. The embroidered bag and the lining should be the same length.
- Run two rows of gathering thread through both the lining (you will stitch through the pockets) and the bag approximately 1cm (1/2") away from the cut edge at the bottom of the bag
- Gather slightly.
- Using a thread which matches the background fabric, and a sharp needle, stitch by hand, the outer base (which you prepared earlier), to the bag approximately 0.5cm (¼") below tack line QR.

- Turn inside out and place the padded inner fabric lined circle over all the raw edges and stitch in place.
- Between the two rows of hem stitch withdraw the threads.
- Cut or make two pieces of cord 60 cm (24 inch) in length. From the centre front of the bag, (not the sides as this will weaken the bag) thread a cord through your channel going over and under two groups of hemstitched threads. Tie ends together. From the opposite side of the bag repeat with a second piece of cord.

Marvellous! Your bag is now complete. Now to the accessories.

Accessories:

Returning to the second fat quarter (page 97), the following items are marked:
- Outer base of bag (Now completed)
- Scissor cushion
- Needle book
- Pin Cushion

Neaten cut edges to prevent fraying.

Prepare and embroider the scissors cushion and pin holder before cutting out.

Needle Book

A longish piece of fabric is required for the needle case as the lining and the embroidered section are one.

Preparation

- Cut out a piece of fabric 34cm (13$^{1}/_{2}$") long and 10cm (4") wide, neaten edges.
- Mark the centre vertically and horizontally, tack lines AB and CD using a #26 tapestry needle and contrasting tacking thread.
- Tack 1cm ($^{1}/_{2}$") in on all four sides of the needle case. This is the seam allowance.

Handy Hint

Stitch the needle book in a smaller frame

Needle Book

each line on chart represents one thread

⊥ *Indicates end of each satin stitch*

▦ *Satin stitch - Watercolours 'ruby'*

▦ *Kloster block - Watercolours 'ruby'*

✳ *Square eyelets - Perle 8 'royal blue'*

▨ *Double Cable - Perle 8 'royal blue'*

- Fold in seam allowance on the two narrow edges, tack down then press.
- Fold one turned edge to the centre tack line AB - on this folded edge run tack line EF.
- Repeat with second narrow edge to form tack line GH.
- Find the centre of the front (shaded area AEFB) and run a final tack line over and under 4-threads to form I J .

To Start

Satin Stitch & Kloster Blocks

Centre the Satin stitch motif and stitch using Caron Watercolours 'ruby' and a #22 tapestry needle. Begin work with a waste knot. Still using the same thread work the kloster blocks.

Eyelets

Use a #24 tapestry needle, Perle #8 'Royal Blue'.

Diagonal Double Cable

Work using the same needle and thread used for the Eyelets.

Back Stitch

To add an attractive finish to the needle case, I worked a row of double back stitch (keep a little tension on the thread) along the seam allowance tacking line GEFH with a #24 tapestry needle and Perle #8 'Royal Blue'.

To Complete

- Cut iron-on interfacing to fit within the tacked area marked 'back' and 'front'. It should measure 15 x 8 cm (6 x 3¼"). (This will fit just inside the back stitched area). Iron into position.

- Fold in along the tack lines on the two long sides, tack and press.

- Bring the short ends together and with a matching sewing thread, and a sharp needle, slip stitch the ends together. You now have a floppy sort of cylinder.

- Prepare the edges of your flannel. The flannel needs to be cut slightly smaller then the needle case. You might like to add an attractive stitching around the edges of the flannel before sewing it in. I worked Nun's stitch.

- Stitch the centre of the flannel, *one thread to the side* of your slip stitched seam on the needle case.

- Press then slip stitch the top and bottom of the needle book together. Make sure the centre seam matches.

- To add a pleasing finishing touch, cut a piece of cord 26 cm (10") in length. Add this to the back of the needle case. Finish the cut ends - I added a tassel.

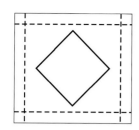

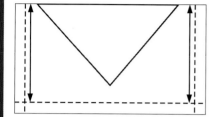

Stitch together through the tack line on two opposite sides, but only stitch as far as the other tack line

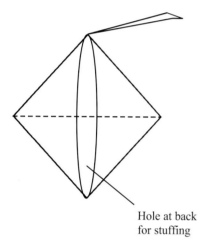

Hole at back for stuffing

Turn work to right side, fold in seam allowance on other two sides, attach cord at one corner, put in some stuffing and slip stitch the opening closed

Scissors Cushion

This is a small diamond shaped cushion.
Preparation: mark out a 10 cm (4 in) square on the second fat quarter.
Run a tack line in both directions to mark the centre point.

To Start

Centre the Satin Stitch over the tacked lines and stitch using Caron Watercolours 'ruby' thread and a #22 tapestry needle starting with a waste knot. Using the same needle and thread work the Kloster Blocks. Eyelets: Stitch with perle 8 DMC 820 'royal blue' and a #24 tapestry needle.

To Construct

• With contrasting tacking thread and a #26 tapestry needle count out from the embroidered area 12 fabric threads and run a tack line. Repeat on all four sides this will be your stitch line.

• With right sides together, fold fabric in half. With a #26 tapestry needle and a sewing thread which matches the background fabric, stitch together through the tack line on two opposite sides only, but only stitch as far as the other tack line.

• Remove the tacking from the stitched sides only. Turn the work through to the right side and fold in the seam allowance on the other two sides. Cut a piece of fine cord 20 cm (8in) in length, fold in half and attach at one corner

• Fill the cushion with dacron or unspun wool and slip stitch the opening closed on the folded edge (seam line) using matching sewing thread and a sharp needle. Loop on to one handle of your scissors.

each line on chart represents one thread

⊥ *Indicates end of each satin stitch*

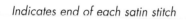 *Satin stitch - Watercolours 'ruby'*

 *Kloster block - Watercolours 'ruby'*

 *Square eyelets Perle 8 - 'royal blue'*

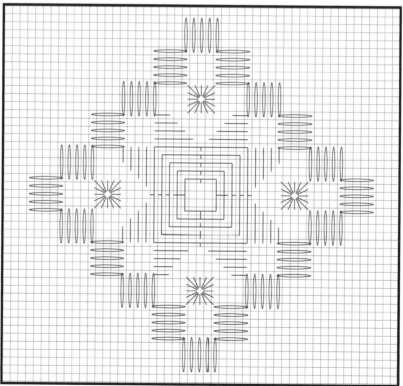

Scissors cushion

Pin Holder

This is made with two pieces of embroidered fabric each of which is laced over stiff card. The two pieces are then stitched together with wool batting in between.

Preparation

Cut out two circles 8 cm (3¼") in diameter from firm card. Place on your embroidery fabric and mark out two circles. Firstly with your HB pencil and then by tacking along the pencil line using a contrasting thread. Find the centre for each circle of fabric. Allow a 2.5cm (1") seam allowance. With the pencil marks on the wrong side embroider the design on both pieces of linen see page 97.

Pin Holder

each line on chart represents one thread

⊥   *Indicates end of each satin stitch*

    Satin stitch - Watercolours 'ruby'

    Kloster block - Watercolours 'ruby'

    Square eyelets - Perle 8 'royal blue'

    Double Cable - Perle 8 'royal blue'

To Start

Satin Stitch & Kloster Blocks

Stitch centre Satin Stitch motif first, then the Kloster Blocks with Caron Watercolours 'ruby' and a #24 tapestry needle. Start with a waste knot.

Cable Stitch & Eyelets

Cable stitch and Eyelets are both worked using Perle 8 #820 'royal 'blue' in a #24 tapestry needle.

To Complete

- Take the two 8 cm (3¼") cardboard circles and glue batting to one side of each card circle. When the glue has set, trim off excess batting at circle edges.

- Cut out the two embroidered circles remembering to add a 2.5 cm (1") seam allowance. Run a gathering thread around each fabric circle.

- Place padded side of card circle to the wrong side of the embroidery. Take care at this stage to match the centre of the embroidery to the centre of the card. Pull up the gathering thread and lace across the card to help keep firmly in place.

- Place both (now laced) embroidered circles, wrong sides together with a small piece of wool batting between them.

- With the thread of your choice and a sharp needle, satin stitch through both circles twice at the same point. Buttonhole stitch over these two threads once. Slip along through the back of one circle to the next point approximately 0.5 cm (¼") around the edge and repeat the stitching together of the circles in this way until you have worked right round the circle. To finish this section of the project, incorporate a pearl-headed pin within each space formed by your stitching. This makes a most attractive and colourful pin cushion.

Place it in an obvious position and wait for the compliments!

With the completion of the accessories your work bag is now complete!